PREPARE IN THE WILDERNESS

RICHARD L. ESLINGER

SERMONS FOR
ADVENT, CHRISTMAS,
& EPIPHANY

C.S.S. Publishing Company
Lima, Ohio

PREPARE IN THE WILDERNESS

Copyright © 1984 by
The C.S.S. Publishing Company, Inc.
Lima, Ohio

All rights reserved. No portion of this book may be reproduced or utilized in any form or by any means, electronic or mechanical including photocopying, without permission in writing from the publisher. Inquiries should be addressed to: The C.S.S. Publishing Company, Inc., 628 South Main Street, Lima, Ohio 45804.

4856/ISBN 0-89536-680-0   PRINTED IN U.S.A.

*To my wife Elise,
for her caring, support,
and covenant love.*

Table of Contents

Introduction			7
Advent 1	*Isaiah 63:16—64:8*	*Advent: Lament, Repent*	9
Advent 2	*Isaiah 40:1-11*	*Marduk? or Yahweh?*	15
Advent 3	*Isaiah 61:1-6, 8-11*	*Good News, Release, and Comfort*	19
Advent 4	*2 Samuel 7:8-16*	*House-Building Time*	25
Christmas Eve/ Day	*Isaiah 9:2-7*	*Come, Celebrate! Send in the Light!*	30
Christmas 1	*Isaiah 61:10—62:3*	*We May Have to Change Our Name*	35
Epiphany (January 6)	*Isaiah 60:1-6*	*Come Home!*	41
Baptism of Our Lord (Epiphany 1)	*Genesis 1:1-5*	*Mary Ann Was Born Again*	45
Epiphany 2	*1 Samuel 3:1-10*	*When God Almighty Speaks... Listen!*	50
Epiphany 3	*Jonah 3:1-5, 10*	*Whom Do You Sit East Of?*	55
Epiphany 4	*Deuteronomy 18:15-22*	*Will the Real Prophets Please Speak Up?*	61
Epiphany 5	*Job 7:1-7*	*"Job" Is Our Name Too*	67
Transfiguration	*2 Kings 2:1-12a*	*Behold! Chariots of Fire!*	73

Introduction

These sermons for the Year B Advent/Christmas/Epiphany cycle have not yet been preached, and in that sense they are not yet full "sermons." Faith comes from hearing, Paul admonishes, and a sermon is not a literary, but an oral, medium. These sermons, then, should be considered more as working documents that in the preaching will image the Word out of the lived experience of a particular community of faith. Specific parishes were in mind during the development of these sermons, so that the images and illustrations may need to change as that congregational context changes.

The liturgical context which is assumed is that of the Sunday service of Word and sacrament; therefore, the sermons draw on eucharistic images wherever that has seemed exegetically and theologically appropriate. But even if the Eucharist is not celebrated each Sunday within your tradition, the Holy Meal is still central to our identity as the Body of Christ, and preaching should point to that reality as it proclaims the Gospel. A specific liturgical context is also assumed for the sermon for the Third Sunday in Advent. Because of the anointing imagery in the lection and its focus on healing, a service of anointing the sick is anticipated in the sermon.

Most of the sermons grow out of a homiletical method which seeks to identify the structure and theological movement of the lection and lets that sequence inform the "homiletical plot."[1] In two instances, however, a type of storytelling methodology has been adopted.[2] For the Baptism of Our Lord, a contemporary story is told which seeks to have congruence with the intention of the day and the lection. The Jonah sermon goes beyond the appointed pericope and attempts simply to tell the story of Jonah. What would not be appropriate in any case would be a topical approach to preaching which ignores the movement of Scripture in favor of a rationalistic and discursive homiletical style. God's Word forms in the hearing of the faithful as a sequence of interrelated movements. The sermon is a dynamic event and not a static collection of ideas. These sermons attempt to express the eventfulness of the Word.

Grateful appreciation is expressed to my faculty colleagues at Duke Divinity School, the Reverend Candice Y. Sloan, and the Reverend

---
[1] Eugene L. Lowry, *The Homiletical Plot: The Sermon as Narrative Art Form*, Atlanta: John Knox Press, 1980.
[2] Edmund A. Steimle, Morris J. Niedenthal, Charles L. Rice, *Preaching the Story*, Philadelphia: Fortress Press, 1980.

Richard D. Waters who showed me the dramatic nature of the Book of Jonah.

Advent 1
Isaiah 63:16—64:8

Advent: Lament, Repent

Israel had much to lament. It was a season for lamentation. The results of God's anger were everywhere. The destruction is easy to catalog:

Holy cities, become a wasteland.
Zion, become a wilderness.
Jerusalem, a desolation.
That "holy and beautiful house,"
The Temple, burned by fire.
"And all our pleasant places have become ruins."

Living in the midst of this wasteland called for an incredible patience before the Lord — waiting for deliverance, waiting for return, waiting for restoration. This patience tested faith, until the lament finally turned to a call for vindication. "God, it is time to turn on the nations in vengeance. It is time for waiting to end and God's wrath to come down."

There is a time for all of us when patience comes to an end, when the frustration finally builds to the point that God must do something. A time comes in life when we have been oppressed long enough. So we call down God's wrath on our enemies. Our prayer changes from a lament to a plea, a demand — "God, make yourself known to your enemies." "Act, God, as you did of old." "O that thou wouldst rend the heavens and come down." And honestly, now, there is quite a collection of oppressors who deserve the wrath of the Lord. Those ungodly, who daily mock God.

Finally, we get fed up and ask for God to act.

It used to be that pious Christians prayed every day for the conversion of Russia. Theirs were fervent prayers, motivated by a deep compassion for those who did not know Christ. But look what all that praying got us. The Red Army invades Afghanistan, Russian tanks once more crushing freedom. Flight 007 strays over Russian airspace and is blown out of the sky. Poland is forced to move against the stirrings of freedom and we watched Solidarity repressed amidst the absurd rationalizing of the military "newscasters." No, we once prayed for the conversion of Russia, but now we would prefer their destruction. It is an evil empire and deserving of God's wrath.

There was also a time when we piously prayed for the church and Christians everywhere. "For the whole state of Christ's church," we prayed. But in recent years, the church, too, has become a battleground. It seems that there are as many enemies inside the church as "out there" in the world. The churches seem like armed camps these days. Factions spend most of their time fighting each other rather than being the church. We open our church newspaper and look at the letters to the editor. The issues may be abortion, the inclusive lectionary, or homosexuality, But the underlying issue is that each side sees itself as oppressed. They are righteous, and the opposition is the enemy. The writers of those letters express Isaiah's frustration perfectly. God will come down in judgment on those who mock God, and the sooner the better! In the church, too, there are enemies who deserve the wrath of God.

We also have more personal enemies: those who persist in attacking us. Sometimes the attacks are designed, like a lawsuit or something. But most of the time, our enemy attacks us just by *being*, and *thriving* — driving a better car, making more money, and (probably) cheating on the IRS. Finally, after repeated attempts at prayer for an enemy, it is refreshing to let loose and pray with Isaiah, ". . . make thy name known to thy adversaries." In frustration, anger even, we call down God's wrath on our enemies.

But Isaiah insists that if we are going to be honest about our enemies before God, we must also be honest about ourselves. We, too, have sinned and provoked God's anger. "We have become like those over whom thou has never ruled," Isaiah confesses. We have become the enemies of God. So all of a sudden, a most surprising thing has happened. The wrath we have called down on our enemies has fallen on ourselves. The adversaries of God include us, the chosen. What a cosmic reversal! God's own people . . . enemies of God!

Now the nature of this covenant guilt is very clear, Isaiah proclaims. It is not hard to understand how we have become God's adversaries. The covenant people are unclean. They are sinful. And they have forgotten God. The first may be the hardest for us to honestly confess. Being unclean is rather foreign to most of us today. We don't think of foods as unclean. A crab cake or lobster is gourmet heaven, not hell. And the disease of leprosy arouses feelings of pity more than a theological judgment concerning cleanliness. But from time to time we do come across situations which immerse us in the unclean.

On a vacation in an unfamiliar area, you stop at the only motel with a vacancy sign. After checking in, you get the car parked, collect the kids and wrestle the luggage to your room. As the door opens, that sense hits you . . . that this is not right. That feeling is confirmed as you enter: the sign on the TV advertising "Triple X" movies, the mirrored wall behind the bed, the red satin cover on the bed. A few minutes ago you were driving down the interstate. Now you are in someplace unclean. For Isaiah, Israel had become unclean before the Lord, like a polluted garment. And when a piece of clothing becomes that fouled, it is usually discarded. The covenant people have become unclean like that, and blessing is impossible to deserve. The unclean are deserving only of God's wrath.

". . . In our sins we have been a long time, and shall we be saved?"

Isaiah is also honest to God about our sinfulness. We are adversaries of the Righteous One because of our sin. Our iniquities "take us away," Isaiah confesses. They have power over us. They control our lives. At this point, though, most of us want to add some restraint to Isaiah's confessions on our behalf. "Look, prophet, maybe I'm not a saint, but I sure am not the worst person in the world!" We can easily think of worse sinners right in this room. Maybe right in the same pew! As a matter of fact, some of us habitually carry around a mental list of sinners certified to be worse than we are. (That's a good list to rehearse when you start feeling guilty about something.)

But it is true, most of our iniquities are not in the category of what used to be called "mortal sins." No, for us it's more "the things we have left undone" that mean that "there is no health in us." Especially in the silence of God's people is our sin disclosed: the awful silence of the righteous; our inaction in the face of the world's injustice; the weekly news magazine, recently arrived, falling open to a full-page photo of a starving child staring out at us (so that we quickly turn the page to the new-car ads).

If we are honest, as honest as God's prophet insists we be, we are sinners. By what we have done, and especially by what we have not done, the anger of the Lord is justly provoked. Our sin has power over us and controls us.

"... In our sins we have been a long time, and shall we be saved?"

One other dimension to our guilt is confessed by Isaiah. He adds that no one calls upon the Lord's name. Or, if we do, we should add, it is only on behalf of ourselves. There is a self-centeredness today that infects us all, sisters and brothers. Our prayer life in shambles, we are mainly concerned about security and what we can possess next. And it infects our churches, too. The way we talk, it sounds to the world like our denomination is more important than Christ's church. There they are — Southern Baptists, Presbyterians, Lutherans and Methodists, of all persuasions — standing around, beating their chests, and snarling at one another. What a family! Self-centered, calling upon their own names, deserving the anger of God. If we are honest with one another, our confession must be that of Isaiah. "... In our sins we have been a long time, and shall we be saved?" The judgment we wished for our foes is upon us — *us,* chosen of God.

What if, on this first Sunday in Advent, our God would "come down" as we have prayed? As we sang "O Come, O Come Emmanuel" and thought of a manger scene, what if were visited by the Ancient of Days? We lit the first candle on the Advent wreath, but did not think of the consuming fire of God's anger. Our thoughts leap ahead to evergreens, while the more appropriate sign this day is a barren fig tree. Isaiah's question remains at the center of our life together —

> "... *In our sins we have been a long time, and shall we be saved?*"

How, then, shall we be saved? It is a good question. Clearly we cannot save ourselves. We cannot quench the wrath of God with a sudden burst of holiness. No, self-justification always just makes matters worse. The only thing to do, Isaiah insists, is to hand ourselves over to God's mercy.

> *Yet, O Lord, thou art our Father, we are the clay and thou art our potter.*

We sinners deserve no more from this potter than to be returned to the earth. Ashes to ashes, dust to dust — and to mud. But listen! What if we gave our misshapen clay back to our potter God? No strings, no conditions, just trusting in the mercy of our Father. The clay of our lives and the clay of our life together, back to the one who created us. Remember Jesus kneeling down, spitting into the dry clay, making clay and putting it on the eyes of a man born blind? The command: "Go and wash"? The cure? It may be in God's mercy that we may be reshaped into new clay for healing. Opening the hospital room door, walking across that polished floor, to the bedside of someone who needs God's love expressed through us. Those people in those beds of pain need that love today, and tomorrow, and tomorrow. So reshape us, God, into healing clay.

Remember Jesus feeding the multitudes? The meager loaves and fishes transformed into a miraculous meal? Maybe, in God's mercy, our meals together as a church people can be an occasion for joyful service rather than silent guilt. What if an empty beanpot were silently present at each church supper, to be filled with contributions to alleviate world hunger? It just may be that our potter God can transform us into a vessel of blessing for the poor of the earth. So reshape us, God, into caring, bountiful clay.

Remember Jesus, gathering his followers around him, taking the bread, and the cup, giving thanks, breaking the bread, and sharing it with them? The command, "Do this in remembrance of me"? Becoming one body, just as we are sharing one loaf? It may be in God's mercy that all these very separate little self-centered bits of clay can be reworked; made into one cup, and one plate;

fashioned into vessels worthy of the presence of the unity in Christ's Spirit, so that the world might believe.

So reshape us, God, into humble earthware that will receive the gift of our heavenly Lord. Come down, Lord God, not for wrath, but for mercy's sake. In the name of Jesus, save us now.

Advent 2
Isaiah 40:1-11

Marduk? or Yahweh?

The prophets had been right. All along, they had proclaimed that it would end up this way. If Israel would not turn to the Lord, would not repent and live justly, an awful judgment would come. The smashing fist would be Nebuchadnezzar, King of the conquering Babylonians. But within the blow of this withering attack was the wrath of Israel's own God. And now the prophesied judgment was upon them. Resistance had been futile, the Holy City was overcome, and the people taken off into exile.

Signs of that holy warfare were everywhere. No one could get away from the evidence of Yahweh's judgment on Judah. There was no denying the bitter fruits of Israel's sins. For those who remained behind, the signs were poignant and dear. The Temple of the Lord, where the swallows once nested, was now a ruin. Its pillars now looked like the tree trunks of a cut-over forest. In the streets of Jerusalem, scrub brush grew tall in the streets, its leaves rustling in the dry wind. The walls of the city had been a metaphor of the glory of Zion, but now they spoke a parable of the irony of a people chosen for judgment. Jerusalem looked like the morning after.

The other sign of God's wrath was the condition of God's people . . . those who had been taken into exile. Things were certainly a lot better there. The city of Babylon was a busy center of commerce, and Jewish shops now joined those of the Babylonians, Arameans, and Medes. And the constant public works projects which seemed destined to put a temple on every corner kept the people busy — and fed. There was not real oppression as there had been in Egypt under Pharoah. But Zion was far off and there was no possibility of even offering burnt offerings to Yahweh for Israel's sin. And in spite of the silly words of the false prophets, the exiles could not return home. Babylon was like a well-kept P.O.W. camp to the exiles: Yahweh's P.O.W. camp for Israel. So the harps were hung up on the willows. It was not a time for singing.

In the midst of this time of trial, Isaiah is told by God to "comfort my people." Speaking tenderly to Jerusalem, Isaiah is to announce that the warfare is ended. Yahweh has declared peace with Israel. The chosen people have more than suffered for their sin. Pardon has been pronounced by their God. Amnesty for draft evaders, pardon for Nixon, and now this: acquittal for a guilty people. Whenever it is extended, grace is a scandal; it is an affront to the righteous. Still, in the silence following this word from the Lord, things don't look much different in Babylon. The canals, the movable gods, the temples — it hasn't really changed.

What *has* changed, though, is everything. Because the Word of the Lord has gone out. It has been spoken by the prophet. It is time to prepare the way of the Lord. In the wilderness, the Lord is coming and this new advent will change history. Those in exile, of course, were already familiar with the kind of preparation the Babylonians made for their various gods. Make a straight path from the gates of the city to the temple and have a triumphal entry. And so every New Year's Day, Marduk is wheeled in procession along the boulevard to his shrine. It's a big thing . . . like the Mardi Gras, Macy's parade, and May Day in Red Square, all rolled into one. Here they come, the temple consorts carrying their pom-pons, following the bagpipes and the fire department float. Israel is familiar with this sort of "way" of preparation.

But another way is also recalled, recovered from Israel's memory. The way in the wilderness, "in the beginning." Out of Egypt. Through the sea. Following the pillar of smoke by day and of fire by night. Water from the rock and manna from heaven . . . and the words "I am your God . . ." Israel remembers this way that the covenant people trod, totally dependent on their God's leading, sustaining guidance. Maybe it's always like that, out of some wilderness. Maybe we just forget and begin to believe that we can just settle down somewhere and live off warm covenant memories.

That is, until some prophet speaks God's Word that deliverance will come through the wilderness. The way will be easy, the rough places a plain, and God's glory will be revealed out here, again, in the wilderness. This wilderness way of Yahweh, begun with Abraham and Sarah, established with Moses, and nearing fulfillment with the Baptist at the Jordan — this wilderness way is now promised to those in exile. And it is Yahweh, not Marduk, who speaks.

Whatever else this Advent is about, it is this: this promise of a way whenever God's people find themselves in some sort of exile, some sort of far country or another. A way for people alienated from God and one another. There are times when foreign powers work to exile God's people, like the persecution of the church in Japan during the Shogun era. But we people of the covenant, we know that most of our "Babylonian captivities" are of our own making. We fill our church walls with newsprint crammed with jargon and flow charts instead of icons and begin to feel a loss of transcendence. And we're in a trivialized church, in exile. Or, we give ourselves to alcohol or drug abuse, or some pet hatred we love to savor, . . . and we recreate Babylon. Or, maybe we just get tired of all the bother and fade away from the scene and wake up later in some far country. Then we cry "all flesh is grass," and acknowledge with the rest of Israel that we cannot save ourselves. We are in exile. And we must come home through the wilderness.

So Isaiah announces this new advent of the Lord God. The One who is coming is mighty. "His arm rules for him." But most appropriate to wilderness passages, Yahweh comes as a shepherd, to gather us together and enfold us, to feed us as a shepherd. Maybe this is why the twenty-third Psalm is so special to us exile people. For whatever else our exile means, it is a time of loneliness and of impoverishment. We find ourselves alone, and without the resources to find our way home, and we are in exile. Like the prodigal sons and daughters . . . in a far country, we need to sing

> *My shepherd, you supply my need;*
>   *and Yahweh is your name.*
> *In pastures fresh you make me feed,*
>   *beside the living stream.*
> *You bring my wandering spirit back*
>   *when I forsake your ways,*

> *And lead me for your mercy's sake*
> *in paths of truth and grace.* *

And the promise of this Word of the Lord is that our Shepherd God will gather us as loved children, giving us times of green pasture and feasting here in this wilderness — not just in the fullness of time, at a heavenly banquet, in Sabbath rest, but now, on our journey. Called from exile, reprieved, forgiven, reunited, and fed, our Shepherd God is preparing the way in the wilderness.

In response, then, we offer the bread and the wine and give thanks. We watch as the loaf is broken, and we receive this bread for the journey. And with all those who have dwelt in exile, but who have now come home, we sing:

> *Holy, Holy, Holy Lord,*
> *God of power and might.*
> *Heaven and earth are full of your glory.*
> *Hosanna in the highest.*
> *Blessed is he who comes in the name of the Lord.*
> *Hosanna in the highest.* **

---

*Quoted in *alive now!*, July/August, 1981.
**The text for the *Sanctus* is from *Prayers We Have in Common*, 1975, International Consultation on English Texts.

Advent 3
Isaiah 61:1-6, 8-11

Good News, Release, and Comfort

Advent rushes to a finish. You know how hectic this next week will be. "Only *(you fill in the blank)* more days until Christmas," and there is an awful lot to be done. There is the last-minute shopping, rubbing shoulders with all the other last-minute people. Then, toward the end of the week, the planning and procuring for the big Christmas dinner begins. But we'll probably forget something essential to the menu and be back at the supermarket on Christmas Eve, too.

Here at church there is as much bustle as there is at home. The choir would love to squeeze in some more rehearsing before the big day, and soon this place will be transformed from its Advent purple to its Christmas white, with the mandatory poinsettias, of course. But other than all that, the checklist of Christmas preparations seems pretty well in order. Or seemed to have been, that is, until Isaiah was read this morning, and a few other items were added. There are now more last-minute things that need to be done before Christmas.

The first of these "additional" items is that we bring good news to the afflicted. One of our Christmas chores is to bind up the brokenhearted. It is a challenging order and has a quite specific meaning. You see, this last part of the book of Isaiah was written after the people returned from exile. They could come home now, but they discovered that, in many ways, they were still hurting.

This restoration was not all it was cracked up to be. Most of the deep wounds that had hurt "out there," away from Zion, now seemed to throb even more when they returned home. You know how it is for a heart patient? Everything seems to be going along all right, and then there is that blow. The pain down the arm, the elephant on the chest . . . all the classic symptoms. And instantly, you are in exile. Maybe you are in the best medical center around, but it's still exile. At first there is nothing but the pain and fear at the center of a whirlwind of medical personnel and technology. The monitor beeping and the I.V. dripping (if they hooked any of *us* up to all that, it would most likely give us a coronary!). But then there comes the move out of intensive care, and a cheery nurse announcing, "Well, we are going to do a little walking today!" (There is something absolutely unique about being in the hospital and that is swinging your legs down and trying to put on that silly-looking pair of new bedroom slippers.) But later, through the grace of God and good medical care, it's going-home time. Exile is over and you are brought to the front door in a wheelchair.

So the time of exile is behind, but there are some surprises — the time of affliction persists, for we are not healed. Now we are a "heart patient." Now we are faced with diet, medicine, exercises — all of it. But this affliction is more emotional than anything. We're angry at being in this situation. Scared it will happen again. Anxious at every real and imagined symptom that our body gives us. So we have gas pains from the lunch, and we focus all our attention on each heart beat. Then comes the frustration — all those things that apparently can never be done again. There's grieving and anger, missing doing them. Hikes up in the mountains, jogging, making love, all of them seem either unachievable or scary. Either way, the affliction continues. Literally and figuratively, we have become brokenhearted. And we need to be bound up. We need good tidings.

That's the way it was for Israel. The exile had been like one great big coronary for God's people. But now they were home . . . and still afflicted. So in all sorts of ways, we too have had our exiles and are now home. We've been afflicted and the wounds still hurt. And that anointing with the Spirit of the Lord is not only needed by Isaiah. We need it too. We need the healing of Christ's presence. Here in Zion, we need the balm in Gilead. So, this Advent Sunday brings us face to face with our own afflictions and those of our sisters and brothers. And it offers us the opportunity for anointing.

For our God wills healing, for Zion and for us.

There is another important item on Isaiah's list of Christmas preparations. Between now and Christmas, we need to be about the business of proclaiming liberty to the captives. The "opening of prison to those who are bound." In the midst of all our other pre-Christmas obligations, the word of the Lord confronts us with this not-so-small matter:

"Proclaim liberty to those in captivity!"

But before we dismiss this message from the Lord as an insane demand, let's think for a minute. What is realistic during these days that will help to release persons from some sort of captivity? What real, concrete decisions can be made between now and Christmas? There are all sorts of captivities we either suffer under or inflict on others, but what about some specific ways in which we can proclaim release?

Maybe if we consider the themes of our Christmas celebration, some of those captivities will become clear. Whatever else, Christmas will be a feast day. After the presents, first come the smells and then the big meal. Ham baked to perfection, mounds of whipped potatoes, those special rolls and the magnificent pies. A symbol of the family holding festival. But for some of us, a sign of captivity; a habit of too much food all the time. A habit may be born of insecurity or deprivation, or may be just a response to people who like to be around "jolly old elves." But it is a captivity no matter how you look at it, and these days are given along with the proclamation that deliverance can be one of the most important Christmas gifts you will ever have. It may start with an anointing to that holy purpose of liberation. Help will be needed, but it's there — from caring people and from our caring God.

Christmas is also a time of the year when more alcohol is consumed than during any other season. Most of it is "social" and some continue to abstain. But if you have become addicted to alcohol, need it most every day, then there is a captivity from which you need release. This is not to point at "the guy in the gutter;" God knows he needs deliverance as well. Almost every family here knows what kind of captivity this is, for most of us either have a friend or relative who is addicted to alcohol, or it is us who are in that captivity. And these can be very important days for those who need release. You can be de-toxified in three days, and by Christmas day be a "recovering alcoholic." Help will be needed along the way, for you cannot do it alone. It may start with an anointing to that holy purpose of liberation. There can be a very special Christmas present this year to your family and yourself.

There is also a wider meaning to oppression. It too is right at the core of our Christmas celebration. For whenever we proclaim the Good News of the coming of the Messiah, we proclaim God's justice and the release of captives. Mary's song, the *Magnificat,* announces what the coming of the Christ child will bring:

He has shown strength with his arm,
he has scattered the proud in the
imagination of their hearts,
he has put down the mighty from their thrones,
and exalted those of low degree;
he has filled the hungry with good things,
and the rich he has sent empty away.

The coming of the Messiah will mean a deliverance for those who are oppressed. Our Old Testament lesson sums it up: "For I the Lord love justice."

Here again the question is: How can we, in this community of faith, respond to the captivity of oppression between now and Christmas? There are probably many ways if we consider prayerfully. But consider this: there is probably no nation on earth that is more open in its racism and oppression than South Africa. The injustice done daily to the majority black population is not even covered up; it's just there for everyone to see. The identification cards, the housing resettlements, the apartheid . . . it's all there out in the open. Between now and Christmas, though, how seriously can we take Isaiah's mandate that we proclaim release to the captives. Well, our trustees could covenant this morning that at the next regular meeting our church trust funds would be evaluated for investments in companies doing business in South Africa. Those companies doing business there could be checked to see if they subscribe to the "Sullivan principles" which a number of U.S. companies have adopted. They promise no segregation or inequality in the conduct of business in South Africa or anywhere else. It's a small step, but one that unites us with our Lord, who announced that he was coming to proclaim release to the captives. There can be a Christmas present from us to those living in bondage. It may start with an anointing to that holy purpose of liberation.

One final item is on the list of Christmas preparations from the book of Isaiah. We are to comfort those who mourn. More than anything else, this comforting of the mourners is a sign of restoration, or redemption. The vision is giving that is fulfilled in Messiah's birth:

> ... *to grant to those who mourn in Zion —*
> *to give them a garland instead of ashes,*
> *the oil of gladness instead of mourning* ...

Israel had returned, but there was still mourning — even in Zion. And now, too, in this place called Zion, mourners abound this Advent Sunday. Some of us have lost loved ones this year and deep down inside is a huge cavern where the joy of their presence once dwelt. And that hollow place is a place of mourning. Some of us have gone through the pain of a marriage that has failed. And that, too, feels like something has died, and we grieve and mourn that loss. Some here, or some related to us, may have known bitter failure in recent days: bad grades at the end of the semester, or a real defeat at work. Whatever it is, important goals are not achieved and we mourn the death of what might have been. Some parents among us suffer with the pain of a rebellious child we love very much, trying to keep a proper face on things before friends, but quietly desperate within our home. We grieve for the child he or she was meant to be, and with God's grace, may yet become. But for now, there is mourning for a son or daughter who is in some "far country" or another. And for some of us, there is grief in just being far from home at this time of year. What is worst, you see, is that for those who mourn, Christmas may just make things worse. It brings back many aching memories, and it isolates us as a little island of grieving in a sea of festivity.

But what is there to do if *all of us* need healing? And, really, isn't that the way this people of Zion are this morning? In some way or another, all of us have been in exile, and even if there has been a return, we are still in need of restoration. And isn't that what this season's about — exactly that sort of healing and restoration? That is why Mary rejoiced in her saving God. This promise of healing and comfort was about to be fulfilled in the coming of a

Messiah. And that promised One would bind up the brokenhearted, deliver the captives, and comfort all who mourn. So the fullness of time is upon us. Now is the acceptable year of the Lord. It is time to build up the ancient ruins and raise up the former devastations. The Spirit of the Lord will anoint us — that is the promise — for healing, and release, and for an end to our season of mourning.

Advent 4
2 Samuel 7:8-16

House-Building Time

The angel was quite clear to Mary. There was no mistaking the meaning of Gabriel's words. Mary had found favor with God and would conceive a child. She was to have a son and call his name Jesus. But this thing which would come to pass became incredibly significant when the angel announced that this child would be given the throne of David. "He will be called the Son of the Most High," and would reign over Israel forever. This son of hers would inherit David's throne. And what is interesting is that Gabriel assumes that this favored one, Mary, knows what it means that her child will be son of David. The promise had been there since Nathan announced it to King David, and now it was coming to pass.

When Nathan the prophet came before David, he reported what the Lord God had spoken to him. David was planning to build a house for Israel's God, but this prophecy took the matter beyond the realm of church architecture. God first reminds David that he has been raised from a shepherd to a prince; it was the Lord's doing that this elevation had occurred.

> Thus says the Lord of hosts, "I took you from the pastures, from following the sheep, that you should be prince over my people Israel."

God has chosen David, chosen him over Saul. And now he presides over the whole of Israel instead of a following of sheep. His name has become great, and, through David, the Lord has established the people in the Promised Land. These honors have already been given to David, but the prophet rehearses them again, because they are only a prelude. All this was just the beginning.

By Mary's time, David had long since become Israel's ideal King. In spite of David's later sinfulness and tragedies, the people looked back to King David's time as the best of times and to David as the greatest of kings. The memory of some of his less glorious successors only made David shine brighter in the eyes of the people.

Something like that happens with us too. We remember some of the recent occupants of the White House and, by comparison, a Washington or a Jefferson become even more attractive. That's the way it was in Mary's time. David and Solomon were the shining stars, but David's shone the brightest. The former shepherd had become the prince of Israel.

The occasion of this prophecy is also announced to David. The prophet Nathan reminds the King of what has already come to pass. Israel has not only been given this "place," this land, but the times of violence are at an end. The Philistines no longer afflict God's people. They are a defeated enemy. Other things have come to pass as well. The Ark of God has come through the times of exodus and wandering, and now finally resides in David's city. And in that city David built many new buildings, including a fine royal palace. So Nathan announces what God has done — he has now given David a time of rest. This lull, this rest, was given so that what was to come could have undivided attention. God gave to David this time of rest. It was given to the whole covenant people as well.

By the time of Mary's encounter with Gabriel, the idea of a God-given rest would have a strange sound to it. True enough, Israel had been given "rest." But it was a state of inaction caused by the triumph of Roman power. The Davidic monarchy had also been put to rest years ago, at the time of the exile. This lethargy which had overcome the covenant could be called "rest," but it was more like "bed rest." It was like being put to bed under doctor's orders, orders issued in Latin. There was covenant rest in Mary's day, but it seemed a lot like being placed in custodial care. It's like a congregation whose membership has drifted away but whose building is preserved for historic value. National Historic Landmarks do have a kind of rest about them. So, there it was: Israel, God's National Historical Landmark, seeming nicely at rest.

But covenant rest is given for God's own purposes. It occurs when the fullness of time has come, when something is coming to pass. And so Nathan declares what God is doing:

"The Lord will make you a house."

David wants to make a house for the Lord, but the reverse is about to occur. God is making a house for David. This is what all that struggle and turmoil was about, the battles with the Philistines and the struggles with Saul. Here is the climax of that whole story. God will establish David's house. The house and lineage of David are proclaimed as God's gift to Israel. "The Lord," Nathan announces, "will make you a house."

For Mary there must have been some irony in this new announcement about David's house. Certainly, there was the dream of a distant time when a son of David would rule again over Israel. But the dream did not have much support in the present. The first citizen of David's city lived in an Imperial palace, filled with social and political goings-on. It was like the American embassy in a poverty-stricken African state — not the best of assignments, but the parties made it more bearable. This promise, though, was still in effect. At the very time when it was coming to pass, all of the signs of the times said that it was null and void. But it had never been retracted by Israel's God. Persisting through all of the ill fortunes of the covenant people, the promise remained: "I will make you a house." Promised in Nathan's words to David, it was fulfilled as the angel spoke in Mary's ear.

Now think about Mary's kind of faith for a moment. We love to sing about the promises of God. Many of us know by heart the words to "Standing on the Promises." Yet it is extremely difficult really to live out of God's promise when all the signs of the times point the other way. We look around and see the vacant pews and wonder if God's promise is empty. We see a lot of congregations merely going through the motions, living out their last days, exercising a presumed right to die.

But watch what will happen. The funeral is finally held after being planned for so long. The for-sale sign is put on the church building. And, not too long afterwards, the church is open once again. New people! They're not of the same denomination, but they're in the neighborhood now and they're coming to the church like mad. They even have a new playground out back for all the kids. Thank God for the promises! God's covenant is established, David's house and lineage continue. "The Lord will make you a house," Nathan says to David. And in Jesus Christ the same grace-filled word is spoken to us.

This word of the Lord is now spelled out for David. Its meaning is expanded. "I will be his father," God declares, "and he shall be my son." The one who will sit on David's throne will be like a son to a loving father. And the one who will reign will speak with the authority of the Lord God. All authority will be given this Son of God. That is the promise. But notice the transformation! We hear the promise and look for a patriarch, some hero like David. Instead, this conceived-of-the-Holy-Spirit one will be born in a humble place, not in the palace. There will be no mighty men of battle to accompany him to victory, only twelve disciples who will desert and betray. We hear the promise and expect someone who will "lord it over us." But this one growing in Mary's womb will say to us that he came to serve and not be served. We hear the promise and expect a patriarch and patriarchy. But the privilege is given to Mary and Mary Magdalene to hear the words, "He is risen." The promise is given, but not as we expected.

And, in spite of the signs of the times, the promise still stands.

There is a further enlightenment given to David. Nathan declares on behalf of God that the son of David will be chastened when needed. If there is iniquity, the son of David will suffer. This had come true, Mary realized. The King of Judah, taken into exile, was punished for iniquity along with all of Israel. Prophets had declared this judgment to a succession of Israel's kings, but there had been no repentance, and a son of David was exiled along with his people. Except, he didn't return, and now David's throne was empty. Mary would think back to a chastening of David's lineage.

Mary would one day think back to another, more immediate chastening, to another, seen-by-her-own-eyes fulfillment. If there is iniquity, then the Son of David will suffer. And another prophet would add, "And with his stripes, we are healed." It's right here in the Christmas story — all those images that point to the Cross. The myrrh of the Magi, "bitter perfume, breathes a life of gathering gloom." The slaughter of the innocents and the flight into Egypt. This one who is born Son of David will suffer, be chastened, on behalf of Israel, on behalf of all of us.

So our Advent joy is not unfettered. There is some restraint to our celebration. Our Christmas observance is not the one going on over at the shopping mall. There is no hint over there, amidst all the tinsel and reindeer and jolly old elves, of the "impending doom" facing the newborn child. So our celebration is somewhat restrained. We bless God for the gift of a son, even as we remain soberly aware that this birth will be difficult for Mary. She will stand before the Cross and know that the Son of David will suffer, be chastened, for the house of Israel.

And a final clarification: this house of David, and of David's line, will last forever. The throne "shall be established forever." The house of King David will never end. In Mary's day, though, it must have seemed to be at an end, or very close to the end. Oh, somewhere there might have been somebody living who was an heir to the throne. But it really made no difference, seeing how Rome was so firmly entrenched. That is a sad thing.

We run into it when we read in the paper about an old lady living in an apartment somewhere in Los Angeles, claiming to be a Russian princess. That is a sad thing too.

But this is not a sad day. For the promise holds. It stands intact for us, for this son born to Mary reigns. God has not taken away that steadfast love. The throne that was established but vacant has been filled. The Holy Spirit has spoken to Mary, and the promise came to pass. The child is born, Son of David, and suffers many things. He dies, "King of the Jews," Son of David. And, after all is said and done, he is our risen Lord. So we gather in this house to witness to that promise, made when Nathan first addressed David: "David, you are going to have a son." And hear it fulfilled when the angel spoke to Mary:

> *He will be great and will be called*
>   *the Son of the Most High;*
> *and the Lord God will give to him*
>   *the throne of his father David,*
> *and he will reign over the house of*
>   *Jacob forever;*
> *and of his kingdom there will be no end.*

Christmas Eve/Christmas Day
Isaiah 9:2-7

Come Celebrate!
Send in the Light!

It was a time of growing darkness for the covenant people. There was not much light in sight. Israel, the northern kingdom, had fallen to the Assyrians and now they threatened Jerusalem itself. Isaiah had pointed to these disasters as sign of judgment from Yahweh, the Covenant God. But the people learned nothing from all the disasters. With nothing but tiny Judah and David's city left unconquered, it only seemed a matter of time. It was a time of growing darkness. And to the people walking in that darkness, Isaiah now proclaimed the coming of a great light.

We are gathered this Christmas *[Eve, Day]* to celebrate the light. In a world that rivals Isaiah's for darkness, we have come together as a people on whom the light has shined. John was right: "the light shined in the darkness and the darkness has not overcome it." For God has come to save us.

Our worship *[tonight, today]* is filled with this light, filled with this joy. More candles are ablaze on Christmas Eve than on any other night of the year, and at the heart of the Advent wreath the Christ candle burns triumphantly.

The people who walked in darkness have seen a great light.

Even from outside, in the dark of Jesus' birthnight, the glow of every Christian worship place can be seen. And, for those who have eyes to see, Isaiah's metaphor is proclaimed again: God has caused a great light to shine on those who dwell in a land of deep darkness.

But it is important that we are not deceived who worship here, in the midst of all this light. We still dwell in the land of deep darkness — maybe even darker than in Isaiah's day. As a matter of fact, this is not the brightest of times.

Out there, in that darkness, there are African children who will die of starvation before our next Christmas celebration. The tribal hatreds run so deep in Northern Ireland, the mid-East, and Latin America, that this special *[night, time]* will only mean a moment's pause in the killing. There is real darkness out there, and at the heart of that darkness are missiles waiting in their deep silos, their consoles emitting a glow as the computers click off the seconds and the minutes of this Christmas *[night, quiet]*. And there is that glowing button, at the bottom of this world's darkness, with the threat of an end to the present, the past and the future. Yes, make no mistake, that is not the new creation out there . . . it is dark, and this light flames distinctly, *in spite of the signs of the times.* For the light shines in great darkness.

But *[tonight, today]* we know that the light *does* shine, and so we rejoice before the Lord. This is a *[night, day]* of joy for God's New Israel. This time of celebration is for us a "harvest joy," as Isaiah foretold. There has been festivity in our midst. There have been family reunions. Our community spans the generations *[tonight, today]* from infants to the elders among us. The "family of God" is rejoicing *[tonight, today]*. Most of our cares are left behind. Why, the finance committee is even putting aside arguing about the budget *[tonight, today]*! For our God has increased our joy. And we have rejoiced before God.

There is a special kind of anticipation, too, in this service of praise. After the Advent time of waiting, the dam of expectation breaks and our voices flood the room with joy. "O Come, All Ye Faithful, Joyful and Triumphant." Every stop on the organ is out, the children's choir is singing like the angels of that holy night, and when we finish singing one carol, we check our bulletin to see when we can sing again. Now we all know that our culture has been celebrating their "Christmas" for a long time now. K-Mart has been playing Christmas carol music for weeks, and the blue light moved to the Christmas ornament aisle after it had been converted from the Halloween display. For months now, it seems that our culture has been pouring sentimental Christmas syrup over us. Now we know *[tonight, today]* that all that stuff wasn't really Christmas —

some ad agency's version, maybe; but it wasn't Christmas — because there was no waiting. In the K-Mart version there's no expectation, no Advent waiting. But for those of us who have lived in darkness, who have waited, expecting the light, this is a joyful time. And it's a joyful time for all God's people. All of us who have been grafted on to Jesse's shoot now celebrate this increase of joy, the birth of the Son of David. Moravian trombones join with choirs singing spirituals while Hispanic faithful celebrate los Posadas.

It is a joyful time.

Now the "why" of this joy needs to be clearly proclaimed. It is not just because we are here and feeling a warm glow. God has done a great thing this *[night, day]* in the birth of Christ. The yoke of our burden and the rod of our oppressor has been broken. The battle against everything that oppresses and burdens humanity has been won in Jesus Christ. That's what this time is about. It is a victory celebration. Isaiah was right: the power of the oppressor has been broken, and the vision is given that one day our task will simply be to clean up the battlefield debris. In our personal lives, all the fear and anxiety and insecurity, all those heavy yokes, have been broken in the advent of this Son. The promise this time is that our joy will be in just cleaning up our personal battlefields of all that debris: the old liquor bottles, the spilt tranquilizer bottles, the scattered divorce notices — stuffing it all into big plastic garbage bags to be taken out with the Christmas wrappings and tissue paper. *[Tonight, today]* the prophetic Word is that all those yokes of ours are broken by God. And it's time to begin cleaning up the place.

It's also a promise that has no bounds, no limits. Every oppressor's yoke will be broken. All injustice will be judged in Christ Jesus. *[Tonight, today]* we finally know that there is no moral power in oppression. The dictators of this world cannot be justified. Their oppression will end, because God has spoken in the coming of Jesus. The yoke of oppression will be lifted off every shoulder. Do you see the vision, church? That the world's babies will have stomachs bulging with good food and not air? Do you hear the promise, people of God? That Latin American torture centers will be turned into well-baby clinics? Do you see the vision, people of Shalom? That a contest will be held by the states to come up with the most creative use for all those old, empty missile silos? The yoke will be broken, Isaiah proclaims. The rod of the oppres-

sor, shattered. And our Christmas joy will be to clean up all those battlefields where war was once waged. It will be like cleaning up around the tree on Christmas morning. With great joy.
Why this great joy? We know why.

"For unto us a child is born. Unto us a son is given."

Not where we had expected. Not as we would have had it happen. But in God's own way. And so we stood a moment ago and heard of God's way. In Bethlehem, of a betrothed couple, . . . humble, faithful folk. And the shepherds, not the most outstanding members of the community, hearing of the news first. The angelic chorus, the sign, the Gloria in excelsis Deo. And then the visitation, the wonderment of all that had happened . . . and Mary, keeping all these things, pondering them in her heart.

"Unto us a child is born."

And with the shepherds we have returned, glorifying and praising God for all we have heard and seen.
There is one other reason for rejoicing *[tonight, today]*, Isaiah tells us. This child, this Son — the government shall be upon his shoulder. You know the titles of this honor: "Wonderful Counselor, Mighty God, Everlasting Father, Prince of Peace." But do you know what this means? It means that the Son of God reigns over the whole creation: over the stars and galaxies and nebulae . . . And, you know what? Even over our enemy out there in the darkness. You know: the one who threatens us simply by being, by existing; who is the object of our anger; who has no right to continue living in such a godless way. That enemy of ours. Calling our values into question like that. Well, sisters and brothers, we are celebrating the birth of God's Messiah *[tonight, today]:*

Wonderful Counselor . . . Mighty God.

Prince of Peace.

And of the increase of his government, and of peace there will be no end.

He will reign forever and ever, over all those enemies out there. And over those enemies deep down inside ourselves. And there will be peace. All will be fed by the bread we break. The cup of blessing will be for us and for all peoples. For to us a child is born, to us a son is given.

And of the increase of his government, and of peace there will be no end.

Christmas 1
Isaiah 61:10—62:3

We May Have to Change Our Name

You can find them in almost every big, old downtown church: the pictures of the pastors of that congregation. They are lined up in a rogues' gallery of clerics. And they look down at us over their names and dates. As you walk down the hall and move back through the decades, some things are easy to notice. The collars get out of date, and then simply strange-looking. Sideburns march up and down as if matched to the stock market cycles. Above all, the farther back you get, the sterner they look in those stiff collars. Religion must have been a sober project back there in the "gay '90s." And have you ever thought, as you looked at a particularly-forbidding saint, "I wonder how he ever celebrated Christmas"?

Scene One

The question is an appropriate one today, on the first Sunday of Christmas. The celebration began on Christmas Eve and this Lord's Day the festival continues. The spirit of the day is set by all that biblical rejoicing we have heard. Simeon, that righteous and devout man who was looking for the consolation of Israel, took the infant Jesus in his arms and sang a hymn of praise:

> Lord, now lettest thou thy servant
>   depart in peace,
> according to thy words.

*For mine eyes have seen thy salvation
which thou hast prepared in the presence
 of all peoples,
a light for revelation to the Gentiles,
and for glory to thy people Israel.*

And there was the prophetess Anna, remaining in the temple, "worshiping with fasting night and day" — "coming up at that very hour" and "giving thanks to God." The season of Christmas is a time of rejoicing, of giving thanks to God for the gift of a savior who is Christ the Lord.

Isaiah, too, has a part in all this Christmas celebrating. As we listened to the first lesson, it seemed as if he was giving us the joyful script for our Christmas praise. God "has clothed me with the garments of salvation," he proclaimed. He anticipated a time of being covered with the robe of righteousness. That's a good way to describe this Christmas season. Clothed with the garments of salvation! Joyful garments; no longer sackcloth and ashes. We see these garments quite immediately in the way the *[Table, altar]* is clothed in white. The stoles and banners and hangings are all signs of being clothed with salvation in Jesus Christ. The festival of Messiah's birth is at hand.

But it is important for Christ's church always to remember that there are other garments of salvation which point to Messiah Jesus. The swaddling clothes in the manger were the first sign — poor, humble, peasant garments of salvation, lovingly wrapped around the babe lying in the manger.

There are other garments, too, which point to Messiah Jesus. Have you ever seen a monastic novice take his vows of profession? He lies there, face down, before the altar, wearing that plain robe in which he will be buried. Beginning a life of service and obedience, he is decked out in that "monk's cloth," that garment of salvation. Remember the four church women killed in El Salvador by the right wing death squads? We watched in a kind of angry grief as the television coverage showed the bodies being exhumed from the shallow grave and covered with those blankets — the garments of salvation, their robes of righteousness. Have you ever taken some clothes out of your bulging closet and dropped them in a bag to be sent to *[Church World Service, Lutheran World Relief]*? Did you ever picture them being sorted by volunteer youth groups and shipped to the refugee families around the world? These, too, are garments of salvation. So the first scene of Isaiah's Christmas script places all of us in special clothing this day — festal garments of worship and praise to honor Messiah Jesus, and servant garb to stand with our Lord.

"God has clothed me with the garments of salvation."

Scene Two

For Scene Two in our Christmas festival, Isaiah shifts to a nature image. "As the earth brings forth its shoots," he says, "so the Lord God will cause righteousness and praise to spring forth." Israel's hope is that in the fullness of time, righteousness and praise will grow and blossom. They will spring up as signs of a renewed covenant "before all the nations."

We have a problem with Isaiah at this point, though. The church today has a hard time seeing these two fruits of the covenant as belonging in the same scene. Most of the time, we tend to think of righteousness and praise as belonging to totally different scripts. One script defines the church as involved in the world, concerned about justice, "impacting" all sorts of needy causes. Yet for those engaged in these missions, worship often is viewed as a distraction. It seems irrelevant to what is important. Unfortunately, without the refreshment of praise-filled worship, this plot usually leads to a collection of worn-out, disillusioned saints. Like an army never rotated off the front lines, the battles wear down and thin out the ranks. Worse yet, without the services of worship, the army may begin to think that the struggle is all theirs — and the victories all theirs as well. It is in our praise of the God of the covenant that we confess that righteousness is a gift and not an achievement. The victories belong to the Lord.

But if there is something abnormal in a church which refuses to take time for praise and the "wasted time" of worship, it is equally sad to see a church which never leaves its walls for service to a world in need. Then its praise rings hollow and the people, incredibly, begin worshiping their own image. An early-warning signal of this disease may be sounding when a congregation prints up brochures for visitors, pointing them to the beautiful stained glass, the beautiful organ, and the beautiful crewel-work stitchery on the kneeling cushions; and the visitor looks in vain for some evidence of ministry in Christ's name beyond the beautiful building. The people have lost their way and are worshiping in the "holiness of beauty." They are praising themselves!

But for Isaiah, righteousness and praise will spring forth together. They belong together, and the church is really being the church when they bloom in the same garden. When the civil rights movement began to shake the old foundations in this nation, now some twenty-five years ago, all sorts of folk were surprised to see the insistence on righteousness and the necessity of praise springing forth together. They were never separated, or the movement would quickly have ground to a halt. The people would gather in a church hall for last-minute instructions. The march route would be explained. The target would be designated — a segregated bus station, the court house, city hall. Marshalls would be appointed and the importance of non-violence underlined once more. Then the march would begin, past the sullen groups shouting obscenities. Accompanied by state patrol cars with riot-stick-armed officers. There were the sounds of chants, some songs, but mainly silence along the way — except for the unforgettable sound of marching feet. The procession arrives at its destination. There is a vigil, sometimes a speech or several, and always prayer. And then back to the church in the same disciplined, purposive way. But back at the church, the marchers didn't simply disperse or begin to mill around. It was like Palm Sunday, and the procession entered the sanctuary and the praising began. Whether there were arrests or not, God was thankfully praised. Whether there had been violence done unto them or not, the Lord was praised. The battles not over, still the victory in Christ Jesus was joyfully proclaimed. Righteousness and praise spring forth together in God's garden: the fruits of God's covenant love.

Scene Three

Isaiah shifts our focus for the next scene. Scene three in his Christmas festival is about our identity as God's people. We will be given a new name!

Be called by a new name which the mouth of the Lord shall give.

Why is that? Why a new name? Because a biblical people know that when something, or someone, is really changed, you have to change the name as well. What Isaiah is really saying is that in the fullness of time, God's covenant people will be made new . . . and will have to be given a new name.

It happens all the time, right in front of our eyes, but we may not see the prophetic nature of the change. The multi-colored wings flex and open and soon it alights like a flying flower. And we don't exclaim "Look at that caterpillar!" Its name has changed. Winter's hard grip on the land loosens and the packed ice melts and the streams bubble down the slopes. And the name is changed. Our Lord spoke of a mustard seed, the tiniest of all seeds, which, when planted in the ground, grows to be the largest of all shrubs. And its name is changed.

We don't call new things by names that are old. And when the covenant God changes people, their names change too. So the promise is: "You shall be called by a new name, which the mouth of the Lord shall give." Look at Saul, persecuting the church, driven by self-righteousness and anger. And when his conversion came on that Damascus road, the apostle's name became Paul.

"You shall be called by a new name."

And Paul reminds the Galatians today that all of us Gentiles once had to be named "slaves" — slaves to sin and death. But because of the gift of Jesus Christ, our names have been changed. Sons! Daughters! "Heirs" of the covenant! We who once were no people are now God's people, and that is at the heart of this Christmas celebration.

When this begins to happen, this rebirth of God's people, it may be time for a new name. When righteousness and praise are beginning to spring forth in the community of faith, we may need to take Isaiah's admonition to heart. If we are being changed, conformed more fully to the mind and spirit of Christ, our name may have to change. All across this land, in almost every community, there is at least one church that calls itself "First." Very few that call themselves "Second" or "Third" or "Last." But open the phone book yellow pages and look at the denominational listings. "First Baptist," "First Methodist," "First Presbyterian." All calling attention to themselves, their own priority in accord with the world's standards. But what if righteousness and praise are beginning to spring forth in that church through the work of the Spirit? What if those people are being covered with God's robe of righteousness? They may have to change their name. Right there in front of everybody. To a name that points not to themselves, but to the source of all righteousness. "Covenant," "Redeemer," "St. Paul" . . . that's for the people themselves to decide, prayerfully and with a Bible in hand. But this much is clear: one sign of the renewal of Christ's church in our land could be new signs in front of old churches with new names. Because when you are changed by God's grace, you have to change your name.

"You shall be called by a new name which the mouth of the Lord will give."

One new name is already given. Isaiah's festival concludes with an image of the renewed covenant as "a crown of beauty" held by the Lord — a "royal diadem" in the hand of God. This, too, is a gift of God's grace. It is certainly not our work, nor our achievement.

But as we surround the Table of the Lord, we are given the Body of Christ. And with the gift of our Lord's presence, we are given again the name that proclaims who we are . . . for ourselves, and for the world. We offer the bread and the wine and give thanks. As the bread is broken and shared, we know ourselves once more to be the body of Christ . . . covered with robes of righteousness . . . where righteousness and praise spring forth. We are the body of Christ, the people of God.

Epiphany (January 6)
Isaiah 60:1-6

Come Home!

The twelve days of Christmas are now at an end. The signs are all about us. The scales tell us the weight we've gained. Trash bags have bulged this week too, overfilled with boxes and paper, waiting to be taken away. Christmas trees are lying down, out in the yard, still streaked with some tinsel. The Advent wreathes are packed away with the tree lights, and the remaining Christmas displays seem oddly present. We are returning to "the real world": business, and war, as usual; a world of darkness, and not light.

Isaiah was right in his prophecy. Whatever else, darkness has come over the earth. There is a "thick darkness" which covers the people. For Isaiah, though, it was not just a "general" darkness that he had in mind. There was a very specific darkness which comes only when you live in a place called "not home." The irony was that the exiles had returned home. But they, too, had found that you can't go home again. They prayed Psalms for Jerusalem, but the gates were smashed and the walls were rubble. They sang Psalms of praise to Israel's King, but the monarchy had come to an end. The returned exiles offered Psalms of blessing to Yahweh for the Temple, but it was reduced to a wailing wall. There was darkness in Jerusalem.

It must have been something like the darkness felt by many of the Vietnam veterans. They had longed to come home, counted the days and then the hours. Finally, their exile-time was over and they headed back — those who lived through it. Only they found, over and over again, that things had changed. They had changed, the country had changed. Instead of that longed-for return home, there was darkness: an ironic, special darkness reserved for those whose homecoming is a rude discovery that they will never be "at home" again.

This thick darkness for Israel was not only the gloom of being "not home." Something else was adding to the dark: a sense of waiting. Israel had been waiting a good long time by now — for salvation, for deliverance, for restoration. It seemed that waiting for the day in which the Lord would act had become the norm. Wherever you looked, there were God's chosen people . . . waiting to be set free. In all the places of dispersion, in Babylon, Egypt, in Midian . . . waiting for the Lord. At home in Jerusalem and Bethlehem and all Judea, waiting for the Lord. Israel, it must have seemed, felt like one big hospital waiting room. Except, for Israel no one was sure whether the wait was for death or birth. There was just the waiting.

Some of us know how that feels . . . to wait like that. Some of us have been given the privilege of that burden. We have learned the suffering of patience, longing . . . the unfulfillment of it. In some cases, there was an end-time already built in. There would be the reunion at the end of the semester. We looked up at the circled date on the calendar and expectantly crossed off the days until "the big day." Or maybe we've looked up and heard the words from the doctor, "You'll be out of the hospital in three days." But for others, the waiting is worse, because it is indefinite. You know how that is? The nursing-home kind of waiting; the teenager-on-a-ghetto-street kind of waiting; the "I-don't-know-when-or-how,-but-I-will-return" kind of waiting. Those are the worst kinds. They test hope, strain on it, beat it down. Those times are times of darkness, special "not-home" darkness that seems never likely to end.

There was one other dimension to Israel's darkness. It was the knowledge that many relatives and friends had never come back. When the exile was ended, they had remained in far-off places. And that only added to this feeling of being "not home" in Jerusalem. We can rebuild the Temple, achieve a bit of prosperity, hope for a new shoot from Jesse's branch; but, in spite of this, life is still incomplete. There are family and friends left behind, and what kind of homecoming is it when they're not here too?

Over and over, this sense of incompletion lives on with us. Particularly in these last few decades, we know something of what it was like for Israel. Family and friends "left behind," unable to make it through the years and come home. For some, there is an acquired indecision, a disease-like inability to stay committed to anything. You know those folks. They used to be here, but by now they have been through the "Jesus movement," the Bahai Faith, and most of the schismatic groups splintering off the main line churches. Oh, they're still around, somewhere. But indecision has become chronic, a way of life. They are religious nomads now, and they can't come home. Others seemed to get stuck in a kind of cultural backwater of the 1960s. We hear about them occasionally, worry about how their children are coming along, see them sometimes in their old, beat-up VW van. There they go, like latter-day Shakers, unable to return from some kind of exile. Then, for some of us, there is a relative or friend who is simply off somewhere. Nothing really wrong, just out of touch and away from home. In Chicago, maybe. Or New York. Or San Francisco. Doing all right when she called last summer, but its obvious she won't be coming home.

For all of these exiles, it seems that their names, too, should be carved into that new monument in Washington — that black granite gash in the earth that memorializes the Vietnam war dead. For there are many who won't be coming home and, living or dead, we mourn them all. Without them, we live in a special kind of darkness: Israel's darkness of waiting.

Now in the midst of this darkness, the word of the Lord comes to Israel. A prophecy so divorced from the signs of the times that it sounds crazy.

The Lord will rise upon you . . . His glory will be seen upon you.

The hope is that a light will shine in the darkness. That is what is prophetic: a brightness of God's appearing, seeming even more intense because of the surrounding night. And this glory of the Lord will call back the exiles; they will come home.

There will be signs you will see, when the long night is about to end. The sign will be the light, the sign will be God's light, and the nations coming. "King to the brightness of your rising."

T. S. Eliot says it poignantly:

A cold coming we had of it,
Just the worst time of year
For a journey, and such a long journey:
The ways deep and the weather sharp,
The very dead of winter.

But Eliot traces the Journey of the Magi to their destination. Arriving at evening,

... not a moment too soon
*Finding the place; in ways (you may say) satisfactory.**

There will be a sign of the coming down. "Kings to the brightness of your rising." Then the light will come.

There will be another sign, Isaiah announces. Beyond these kings coming to you, your lost ones will return home as well. These sons and daughters who were lost will return. The outcasts, the sinners, the lost, all of those remaining in exile will be brought home. You know those outcasts: a leper stretching out his hand for cleansing; a man named "Legion" ranting out among the caves; a woman of Samaria seeking living water. You know those outcasts. They will be healed, and forgiven, and restored to Zion. That will be a sign that the darkness will soon pass. It will be a sign that the long night of waiting is drawing to a close.

Oh, yes. There is another sign. One more sign is given that the thick darkness is ending. These exiles and outcasts will come from afar, these sons and daughters. And they will "bring gold and frankincense, and shall proclaim the praise of the Lord." The enduring sign of the new light will be a people joyfully assembling on the day of the Lord, for praise of the Lord. The people, praising their God . . . that will be the sign. Brought together from near and far. Old timers and newcomers. Individuals and families from New England, out West, and down South, they will come together for praise, knowing that the Lord has brought them home. Maybe they come through "dangers, trials, and snares." From sick beds and shattered families, and places where they should not be, they have come. Healed, reconciled, forgiven will be this new family of God. They are the sign that the light has dawned: a sign of praise; a light to the nation; God's people once more brought home.

---
*T. S. Eliot, "Journey of the Magi," in *The Complete Poems and Plays, 1909-1950*, New York: Harcourt, Brace and World, Inc., pp. 68-69.

Baptism of Our Lord (Epiphany 1)
Genesis 1:1-5

Mary Ann Was Born Again

In the early church, three Sundays were reserved for the baptism of new Christians. Except in an emergency, these candidates for initiation into the church were baptized on one of these three days. The Easter vigil was the primary occasion, with its drama of darkness and new light, death and new life. As our Lord made his Passover from death to new life, so the candidates were baptized into Christ's death and resurrection. Pentecost Sunday was the second of these baptismal days for the early church. The Holy Spirit was given at Pentecost and is given by God's grace in Baptism. It is an obvious Sunday for the making of new Christians. This Sunday, the festival of the Baptism of Our Lord, is the third of those days. Because Jesus came to the Jordan and was baptized by John, this Sunday is the anniversary of the baptisms of Christians "in every place and time." It is also the anniversary of the baptism of a friend we'll call Mary Ann. She has been a Christian ten years today.

Our friend had spent all her childhood and young-adult years within the protective walls of one of America's more respectable sects. By orthodox Christian standards, this "church" is clearly a heretical body. But you know how American attitudes are on this sort of thing. If your heresy is expressed in a quiet, proper middle-class manner, "heresy" somehow seems to be too harsh a word. We save that label for Jim Jones' followers, or the Moonies, or similar such groups.

Anyway, Mary Ann had grown up in that conventionally heretical "church." There was no preaching in that denomination, no

Lord's Supper, and she had never been baptized. But in her young adult years, she began to find her church's rather authoritarian answers to life's problems increasingly unsatisfactory — answers to the problems of why there is sickness and pain and suffering in the world. Consequently, the authority of that community's hold on her began to drop away. Soon, like many other people in this country, she would identify herself in a poll as "none of the above."

Now, when the old order in people's lives collapses, sometimes there is outright chaos; severe dislocation; even suicide. We think of the social disorder following the Fall of Rome; of Berlin in 1945; and, more recently, of Saigon. When the old authoritarian order collapses, sometimes there is chaos. For many more people, though, the effects of this loss of old, familiar structure is less dramatic.

That's the way it was with Mary Ann. There was a kind of depression and grieving, very much like somebody close had just died. Part of it was that the old language of her religious background no longer worked. It no longer had power for her. It was all still there, woven into the patterns of her thinking. And yet it was obsolete. It's much like the feeling we get when using the expression, the "four corners of the earth," after seeing photos of the earth taken from the moon. The rituals of her old religion were obsolete as well.

For a time after she "lost the faith," she was still a practicing member of the group. It's interesting how often that occurs. People can go through the motions of maintaining a dead marriage for years. Mary Ann went through the motions of practicing a dead faith for several years at least.

But what was most depressing about the loss of this "faith" was the loss of a community. Her former friends just didn't seem as available as they had been before. It was as if *she* had died, the way she was being treated. She began to realize that, after all those years of participation and investment, her absence had made no difference at all. And that made her angry, too. She felt depressed, grieving, and angry. Not a great place to be. But a place to which most people come one time or another, for one reason or another. Now, however, it was Mary Ann's turn. Her old gods had died, and with them, something in her had also disintegrated.

About that time, she learned about a program in town that

helped the street people and other really "down-and-out" folks. These people seem to collect in certain urban areas, almost as though drawn by magnets. And this particular downtown church sponsored, on Monday nights, a "drop-in center" which provided a nutritious meal and a social time afterwards. A donation of a quarter was asked for the meal, but no one was ever turned away. And the drop-in center staff would circulate among the hundred or so people who remained afterwards. They would join in a card game; referee arguments; but mainly just talk and listen.

Every Monday evening was guaranteed to be hectic and exhausting for the staff: working to get an alcoholic to a detoxification center; trying to find housing of some sort for a couple newly arrived in town but with no money; listening to ten people at once, each with a different problem or issue. Mary Ann enjoyed the involvement that came with serving on the volunteer staff. It gave her something to do, but it also provided real rewards. Isn't it interesting how immersing yourself in other peoples' needs can be so therapeutic? It has a way of healing our own wounds. And some good, old-fashioned caring for other people is probably the best cure for depression ever invented. Mary Ann was discovering that, to her great pleasure!

She was also discovering something else. She was finding out about some Christians as well. There was the church treasurer, for example. He had worked all day in a pressure-cooker job, but here he was, presiding furiously over the big kitchen stoves, cooking dinner for the expected crowd. In the heat his face would take on a reddish hue, and he would complain about things not being where he wanted them. But he'd be there, faithfully cooking up a storm. Several suburban housewives would also be there, pitching in. Their church had no outreach ministry so they commuted in every week to be part of one in the city. Mostly, though, the staff was composed of young adults like Mary Ann. Their social life centered on the drop-in center and the interminable staff meetings, rather than on singles bars and those sorts of things. In the midst of this labor, there seemed to be a spirit, an intensity, compassion about these folks. And the spirit was catching. In fact, Mary Ann had caught it.

Now the rhythm of life for a drop-in center staffer almost necessarily involved joining with the rest of that church community in Sunday worship. Here, in the Sunday service, these troops in the "trenches" could get some necessary "R & R." Concerns were shared in prayer for specific persons and situations at the Center. Special offerings of canned goods were a regular part of the worship. Mary Ann found herself coming to church more and more frequently. She got invitations to Sunday dinner from several of the church families. In fact, it was beginning to feel like she had a new family. Mostly, she was still moved by the lavish presence of Scripture in the service, some read by laity each Sunday. There was preaching (something new for her) and the biblical world began to be opened for her. She learned of mustard seeds, loaves and fishes, and the command to "feed my sheep." And there was a wondering about Holy Communion, and then a growing desire to share in that Holy Meal. She found there was something unfulfilled about worshiping when you felt like part of the family, but had not broken bread with them. She joined in the Prayer of Thanksgiving, listened as the Spirit was invoked on the gifts and the community, and watched as the bread was broken. Then she *watched* (rather than shared in) the Meal. It felt increasingly odd to her not to be fully a part of the family of Christ.

At that point, the meetings with the pastor began. In the early centuries of the church, Mary Ann would have been called a "catechumen," a *candidate.* The sessions did focus on the historic creeds, on Christian doctrines, and on the meaning of the sacraments. But mostly they were discussions that sought for the underlying meaning of the ministry and worship that had involved her so fully. The meetings continued all that winter. Then came this Sunday, the Baptism of our Lord, the Sunday for Mary Ann's baptism.

Following the lessons and the sermon, Mary Ann was escorted to the big marble font by the church lay leader who was her sponsor. The service of Holy Baptism began with a renunciation of the darkness of the world and an affirmation of faith in Jesus Christ. The whole congregation was invited to the renewal of their own baptismal covenant, as well. Then everyone joined in the Apostle's Creed, the earliest baptismal creed of the church. The pastor then offered the prayer of thanksgiving over the water which proclaimed God's wonderful acts of salvation in and through the waters. It began,

*Eternal God,
when nothing existed but chaos,
you swept across the waters of creation
and brought forth life.*

The prayer concluded, invoking the Holy Spirit to bless the gift of water and those who receive it. The water was then poured and Mary Ann was baptized in the name of the Triune God. With the laying on of hands, the pastor said, "The power of the Holy Spirit work within you, that being born through water and the Spirit you may be a faithful witness to Jesus Christ." Then, with the branch of an evergreen, the congregation was sprinkled with water with the words "Remember your baptism and be thankful!" Mary Ann was born into the family of the church. She had come through the Jordan and received the Spirit. It was a day of great joy for the church and for this new Christian. "Christians are made, not born," Iraneus said centuries ago, and he was right.

Oh, and as for Mary Ann, on this tenth anniversary of her baptism? Well, later on she experienced God's call to ordained ministry and went off to seminary for her preparation. She was ordained after graduation and is serving a congregation now. And today, this Sunday of the Baptism of Our Lord, it is quite likely that she is holding an infant in her arms and proclaiming before the community of faith, "I baptize you in the name of the Father, and the Son, and the Holy Spirit. Amen."

Epiphany 2
1 Samuel 3:1-10

When God Almighty Speaks . . . Listen!

Hannah was among the barren women of Israel. She had no children. But Hannah was also among the *faithful* women of Israel. So one year, at the time of sacrifice, she made a vow to the Lord. In the midst of her distress, she uttered a tearful prayer:

> O Lord of hosts, if thou wilt look on the affliction of thy maidservant . . . but wilt give to thy maidservant a son, then I will give him to the Lord all the days of his life.

Later, after the worship and the sacrifice, the family returned home, "and in due time Hannah conceived and bore a son, and she called his name Samuel, for she said, 'I have asked him of the Lord.' " And, true to her vow, Samuel began serving the Lord even as a boy, supervised by the chief priest of the temple at Shiloh.

> Now the boy Samuel was ministering to the Lord under Eli. And the word of the Lord was rare in those days; there was no frequent vision.

It seems an odd context for ministry, but there it was: the boy Samuel, serving old Eli at the Temple, with the word of the Lord grown silent. God's word was "rare in those days." Most everything went along as it has a habit of doing, even without an encounter with the word of the Lord. The activities at the sacred place all continued. It was the site of the Ark of the Covenant in those days, and so certain things needed to be done, even if there was no word. Pilgrimages to the shrine were made, animals sacrificed, rituals performed, to keep undefiled this place of a silent God.

The reason for this silence, the story reports, was right there at the shrine. Eli's two sons had violated God's Torah and done evil in God's sight. So the purity of the word of the Lord was really a judgment, a sign of the wrath of this righteous God.

It seems odd how little some things change. The whole story sounds familiar. People gradually realize that the word of the Lord has become rare. And the problem becomes "God." There is silence from God and the more outspoken observers announce the "death of God." Most of us, though, don't seem to miss the Word too much. We can keep on with all our own words. But have you noticed what's happening? It is *our own words* that are losing their vitality. The signs are everywhere. Have you read a report on an important issue by one of our church agencies lately? Have you noticed that the languages of Scripture and Tradition are strangely absent? And, in their place, the "communication" is bloated with jargon. You will find all the "in" words which important church leaders use to talk to each other: "impacting," "marginated," "prioritizing."

And in the midst of this flood of words, it is sadly clear that the Word of the Lord is rare in these days. It doesn't take long to discover where the words of the tradition have gone. Just turn on the television any evening and stay in the room during the commercials. Our words are being used to sell soft drinks, automobiles, and antacids! Three hundred people somewhat curiously lining a winding road change their chants from "I don't believe it!" to "I believe it" through a Toyota sport coupe's epiphany. The church leaders have taken to talking like government bureaucrats and Madison Avenue sounds more evangelical than Billy Graham.

So guess what the response of the people is to the sickness of words? Repentance? Lamentation? Reformation? Well, not really. The response is a bad attack of religious nostalgia. At this very instant, almost every television channel is clogged with "old-timey" preachers offering the "good old days" in living color! It's a kind of Disneyland version of the old time religion — beautiful, inviting, and sounding almost like the real thing. But in the midst all this language, inside the church, and in the world, the haunting words of Scripture cut through the bubble:

The word of the Lord was rare in those days.

The story now states the barren nature of Israel's relationship to God with a shift in images. "There was no frequent vision." The Lord was not only *not heard,* but *not seen* either. The absence of Israel's God was complete. To round out the picture of barrenness, Eli, the chief priest, was lying in bed next to the temple, his eyesight grown dim so that he could not see. There were no visions, and the high priest was blind! It was night. The lamp of God which had burned all night, had not yet gone out. It was now just before dawn. But it was still very dark, as dark as the vision of Eli, as dark as the absence of God.

You can feel that kind of darkness without going too far from home. Imagine a big church on a downtown street in the middle of the night. The street light down the block only serves to underscore how dark it is inside. Everything is locked up tight, dead-bolted and chained. The only light in the whole building is the glow of the alarm system's panel in the office. Otherwise it is dark, a place of infrequent visions. A figure curled up asleep by the side door is the only sign of life. That's how it is during the night watches — a time of infrequent visions, just before dawn.

Then the word comes. No vision, just a word. "Samuel," "Samuel," the Lord calls, calling Samuel to be prophet and leader of Israel. But Samuel is only expecting old Eli's voice in the night; the call is misunderstood. Three times this call comes to Samuel. There is an insistence about it, the way there was when you used to hear your mother calling you to come home. Over and over your name was called, until you finally answered. The call of the Lord had a commanding urgency about it.

Even if Samuel didn't know the source, he did answer. The phone rings and we jump to answer, not knowing if it is news of life or death, or just somebody selling light bulbs. It compels us to answer. The call was personal, too, not to just anyone.

You are making your way through the crowded concourse in an airport somewhere, and you hear your name being paged. That's how it was for Samuel. He had to answer: the call was to him.

Of course, he was mistaken about who was calling him. Every time the Lord calls, the boy dashes in and wakes up the old priest.

But Eli knows the ways of the Lord. He instructs Samuel to lie down again; but if the call recurs, Samuel is to answer, "Speak Lord, for thy servant hears." So the stage is set for this encounter between Samuel and the Lord.

And the Lord came and stood forth, calling as at other times, "Samuel," "Samuel." And Samuel responded as Eli had instructed, "Speak Lord, for thy servant hears."

The call of the Lord is an awesome thing. It has an insistence about it. Some kind of response is necessary — even if for some of us the response is to pretend to ignore it for another season.

Notice that Samuel had to be called if he was to serve the Lord. There had been all the special circumstances of his birth and childhood. Hannah's barrenness. Her faithfulness and vows to the Lord. Samuel; having being "lent" to God's service. All of that was important. But God called Samuel, and Samuel must respond. "Yes" or "No." Either, "Speak Lord" or, "I won't listen." It's that way when God calls . . . that personal, compelling call to us. All of a sudden, the issues of life are drawn rather clearly. The choice becomes one of saying "yes" or "no" to the future that holds promise of who you are meant to be. And what had been a multiple-choice vocational question is now a forced-choice situation.

We have to respond — to claim the call for ourselves, or to reject it. And so we hear people constantly exclaim how fine our voice is, how professional its quality; but we hear ourselves answering that we are going to enter nursing school — or medical school — in the fall. The top management offers us a "fast track" advancement opportunity. We express deep appreciation but turn it down because of its effect on our family life. The computer readout from the occupational preference testing service comes in the mail. We chuckle as we read that we should do well in the fields of law, marketing, and civil engineering. The form is folded up and the seminary catalog is opened; God is calling us to the ordained ministry.

The call of the Lord is like that. We can wrestle with it; try to close our ears; or, as in the case of Samuel, answer "Speak Lord, for thy servant hears." The call of God is terribly insistent, totally personal, and it is always calling for *us* to respond, "thy servant hears."

Then, there is the vision. The time of infrequent visions had ended. The Lord came and stood before Samuel. Samuel was confronted by the presence of the Holy One of Israel. Dawn had come, for Samuel, for Israel. Dawn comes to us, too. The church building is unlocked, the alarm system turned off. The stranger by the side door is helped up and given some breakfast down in the kitchen. Soon the people start trickling in . . . the choir, minister, organist. The Table is set with a plate and a cup. Candles are lit. The room fills with God's people and the light of this new day, the day the Lord has made. There is joyful praise; the Word of the Lord is heard; and, through God's grace, the vision is given.

The dawn has come. Thanks be to God!

Epiphany 3
Jonah 3:1-5, 10

Whom Do You Sit East Of?

Now the word of the Lord came to Jonah the son of Amittai, saying, "Arise, go to Nineveh, that great city, and cry against it; for their wickedness has come up before me."

Finally the evil of the Ninevites had provoked the Lord God to action. Yahweh had had enough. A prophet was needed who would proclaim the word of judgment to the enemy. Jonah, son of Amittai, was chosen for this mission — to cry out against the wicked of Nineveh. But as we all know, this "prophet" rose to flee from the presence of the Lord.

He went down to Joppa and found a ship going to Tarshish; so he paid the fare, and went on board, to go with them to Tarshish, away from the presence of the Lord.

While Jonah is stowing his luggage below decks, it might be a good time to raise the question as to why he is trying to flee from the presence of the Lord. All kinds of answers have been proposed — a lack of courage; too much pride; a "let's-not-get-involved" mentality. But the Bible doesn't provide an answer. It simply says that he "rose to flee from the presence of the Lord." That's all it says. To be honest, we can't even say why we avoid God's words to us most of the time. Like Jonah, though, we just rise up and flee. And for a while, it seems to work. The boat sets sail, Jonah can relax, and, in fact, he is soon asleep down there in the "hold," as sailors call it. So off he sails for Tarshish.

We all know how far he got. It didn't take long for things to catch up with our prophet. For the Lord "hurled a great wind upon the sea, and there was a mighty tempest on the sea, so that the ship threatened to break up." The mariners were afraid, each crying to his god to save them. They try to lighten the ship by throwing the wares overboard. Then, it is discovered that our hero is sound asleep down there in the inner part of the ship. So the captain hurries to waken him so that everyone can be appealing to the god of his or her choice. It is clear that someone on board is at fault: the tempest is too great to be from natural causes. So they cast lots to see on whose account the evil had come upon them. And the lot fell to Jonah.

Thinking they had better find out about this stranger in short order, a series of questions is fired at Jonah:

What is your occupation?
And whence do you come?
What is your country?
And of what people are you?

Jonah's answer brims with confidence. (He is a prophet after all!) "I am a Hebrew; and I fear the Lord, the God of heaven, who made the sea and the dry land." Isn't it reassuring that we have our religion to fall back on in such times of crisis! But the mariners also learn that our prophet is fleeing from the presence of the Lord, "because he had told them." One thing about Jonah, he can be brutally honest at times. So his shipmates say to him, "What shall we do to you, that the sea may quiet down for us?" For the sea grew even more tempestous.

Jonah could have tried other popular moves for avoiding the will of the Lord. But to his credit he didn't. No, he simply announced: "Take me up and throw me into the sea; then the sea will quiet down for you; for I know it is because of me that this great tempest has come upon you." What nobility! What honor! What sacrifice! Besides, everyone loves a martyr. He can see it already: "Jonah Memorial United Methodist Church."

There was quite a struggle to get back safely. The sailors rowed hard to bring the ship back to land — pulled mightily on their oars: pulled and pulled and pulled. (Interesting, isn't it, how godly these pagan sailors are . . .) And where's Jonah while all this life-or-

death effort is going on? Sitting on a deck chair, reading a soggy old copy of *Yachting Times*.
But it doesn't work! It is to no avail! All is for naught! So the sailors open the *Book of Common Prayer* to the collect for such an occasion, quickly pray the prayer, and throw Jonah into the sea. The sea then ceases from raging and takes a striking likeness to the swan-boat pond in the Boston Commons. And there they are, these now-devout sailors, all fearing the Lord exceedingly, sacrificing to the Lord and making vows. What an ending! What a great sermon illustration this will be! While Jonah sinks slowly to the bottom, these former pagans are all up on deck having church.

Except for one thing: Nineveh. The call was to go to Nineveh and prophesy — not to join those lost at sea. So,

The Lord appointed a great fish to swallow up Jonah; and Jonah was in the belly of the fish three days and three nights.

It is a time for some serious stock-taking, real soul-searching, perhaps even prayer. And from the belly of the great fish, there ascends to the mighty God of Israel an especially pious Psalm of lament. Probably, there are more "fish-belly" type prayers than any other kind — at least of the individual sort.

"Get me out of this mess I got myself into, Lord, and you will have an exemplary servant on your hands."

"God, I have just borrowed my folks' car without permission and wrecked it. If you get me out of this, I won't miss youth fellowship for the rest of the year."

"God, I've over-eaten, smoked too much, and never exercise, but if you let me recover from this heart attack, I'll increase my pledge and cut back on desserts."

Fish-belly prayers. All of them. But this lament bubbling up from the deep is heard by the Lord who speaks to the fish, which vomits Jonah out on the dry land. "Only trust him, only trust him, only trust him now. He will save you, he will save you, he will save you now."

However, there was this matter of Nineveh — this call, this mission, this Word of the Lord. And so, it comes again to Jonah; a second time comes the Word of the Lord:

> *"Arise, go to Nineveh, that great city, and proclaim to it the message, that I tell you."*

Now there is a certain way of walking when the situation gets hot and heavy. It's not a light, expectant gait, but rather purposeful, heavy, "intentional," as some might say; like Stonewall Jackson on a night march. Well, that's how Jonah moved onward to Nineveh after that fish incident. Five miles an hour, rest ten minutes each hour, and then get moving again. There he goes, old "Stonewall Jonah." Marching, not to Zion, but to Nineveh.

There is nothing quite like the fury of God's righteousness, God's prophets. Equipped with this Word that is like a two-edged sword. And even if this particular prophet has not exhibited much righteousness up 'til now, when Jonah sees wicked old Nineveh sprawled out before him, he gets right on with the task.

> *Now Nineveh was an exceedingly great city, three days journey in breadth. Jonah began to go into the city, going a day's journey. And he cried, "Yet forty days, and Nineveh shall be overthrown!"*

Do you know how good that feels, being on a crusade for God? All moral ambiguities are behind and the really bad guys ahead. When you are the one who must do what has to be done — axe a few saloons, seize an embassy, or highjack a plane — well, *that* good is how Jonah feels during the day-long recitation of his dirge, "Yet forty days and Nineveh will be overthrown."

Too bad most of us don't get many of these chances, when all the moral choices are so clear: good and evil identified by uniforms and background music like a *Star Wars* soundtrack. It's too bad, but most of our real moral choices are tough: like those hard medical ethics questions about life-support for the terminally ill. Of course, there are folks in the church who act out of Jonah's undaunted certainty. They scream at each other "Pro-life!" "Pro-choice!" They pass lots of resolutions condemning this and that government action. It's heady business, and a refreshing change from our daily round of choices that more or less reflect God's will. But at least Jonah finally got a chance to speak unequivocally for God against the godless. For one glorious day the prophetic word was hammered home: "Repent or be destroyed."

Unfortunately, they repented.

Well, to say that "they repented" is a bit of an understatement. When the polls closed God had a landslide. *Everybody* repented! They believed God, proclaimed a fast, and put on sackcloth, from the greatest of them to the least. And when the king of that wicked city heard of Jonah's message, he too repented, and sat down in his sackcloth on a pile of ashes. And then the royal proclamation was issued.

> *By the decree of the King and his nobles: Let neither man nor beast, herd nor flock, taste anything; let them not feed or drink water, but let man and beast be covered with sackcloth, and let them cry mightily to God; yea, let everyone turn from his evil way and from the violence which is in his hands. Who knows, God may yet repent and turn from his fierce anger, so that we perish not.*

There are times when people *do* change like that (thank God). Maybe not to the extent of dressing donkeys in sackcloth. But real change. From being toward death to being toward life. Out of darkness into the light. Saul becomes Paul; Augustine turns to God and God's city; Charles Colson gets out of prison and starts working for prison reform. And even in our own church, we are probably blessed by those who have known the awe-full grace of God's word, judgment, and then forgiveness. And with them, all of us sinner/saints praise our redeeming Lord: "Then sings my soul, my Savior God to thee, How great thou art, how great thou art!"

All except Jonah, that is. He is now exceedingly displeased and quite angry as well, because the compassionate God of Israel is gracious and merciful, slow to anger, and abounding in steadfast love. Nineveh is not going to be destroyed. So Jonah now can rationalize his flight to Tarshish: he knew God would repent! And what an embarrassment that would be for a very righteous prophet. As a matter of fact, "it is better for me to die than to live," announces our righteous prophet. Instead of dying then and there, however, Jonah decides on another plan: he'll wait God out. So he strides out of the city, heads east for a bit, and sits down to wait and see what will happen to the city. Maybe God will repent of that repentance!

Have you ever sat to the east of someone — all upset about how awful they are, and how they should not have the right to be who they are? Remember how they threaten you — that enemy of yours. Even by doing nothing, they attack you and your virtue. Remember how your rage felt? The anger, the tension, the distraction . . . the high blood pressure. And today, is there any among us, in addition to Jonah, who are sitting to the east of an enemy, waiting for them to get their just desserts, their come-uppance? Or maybe, with our prophet, simply waiting for them to die?

Out there, in the heat, east of the city, Jonah did not have to wait long for some divine action. For the Lord God appointed a plant, that it might be a shade over his head, to save him from his discomfort which pleased Jonah all that day, until the worm was appointed which attacked the plant so that it withered. And the sultry east wind was appointed, and the sun's beating down was appointed. And Jonah, now angry enough to die because of all this appointing, said to the Lord, "I do well to be angry, angry enough to die." And the Lord said,

> "You pity the plant, for which you did not labor, nor did you make it grow, which came into being in a night, and perished in a night. And should not I pity Nineveh, that great city, in which there are more than a hundred and twenty thousand persons who do not know their right hand from their left, and also much cattle?"

And with the words "and also much cattle" our stay ends. Our little prophet sits, still angry, outside the city — pouting because of their repentance. He's glowing with self-pity because of the plant-and-worm sermon illustration. Later, much later, One will rejoice at repentance, weep over the city, and die outside its walls. It's interesting how little things change though. Not many of us will make it through this week, or even this day, without being confronted by a similar choice — in the presence of our enemies, to say "smash them Lord, really do it this time!" or to pray "forgive them, for they know not what they do."

Maybe the choice is upon us right now . . .

Epiphany 4
Deuteronomy 18:15-22

Will the Real Prophets Please Speak Up?

There was a time in Israel when no prophets spoke for God. During those long years after the Exile, prophecy seemed dead. There were no prophets and none were expected. All the people could do was to look back for comfort to the times when God had sent an Amos, an Hosea, an Ezekiel. Those were the good old days, when the word of the Lord was heard in the land. But now they were gone . . . and the long wait for the messenger of the Lord had begun.

Our problem is quite different, it seems. We may be living in a time when the word of the Lord is restrained. But there is a "prophet" on every street corner. They are everywhere.

We live in a time ridden with "prophets." There is a real oversupply problem, prophet-wise: all of them claim to speak the *real* truth, of the *real* religion, on behalf of the *real* god. We run into them everywhere we look, leaders of one movement or another — the Phil Donahue Show, the evening news, the Religion Section of *Time*. There are the "prophets" of American civil religion, lecturing us on God and country, wearing an American flag in their lapels where a cross ought to be. At the same time, the "prophets" of the religious left are yelling at us too, telling us to get the U.S. out of East Timor and condemning American policies on most everything. The "prophets" of a "feel good today" church charm us with positive thoughts brought from a college campus somewhere that looks like a cross between Cypress Gardens and

Forest Lawn. Wherever we turn, we and our church are accosted by self-appointed prophets, all arguing with each other, and all claiming to speak for God.

Beyond the church, other prophets are also calling for recognition. There are all kinds of other religious groups — more and more of them, it seems. And they all have their prophets. Some sects keep dividing like amoeba, each splinter group led by a "prophet" who is constantly surrounded by big, mean-looking bodyguards all wearing sunglasses. New religions have also sprung up, each with a leader who is revered as a prophet-like figure, come from God. These new cults surprise us with their popularity. There is Yankee Stadium filled to overflowing with people come to hear Rev. Moon prophesy to them. Then there are all the "human potential" movements, offering new ways to become more freed-up and mellowed-out, each one led by a "prophet" of the new wave. Somehow, they all seem to collect on the West Coast and are heralded by the *National Enquirer* at a rate of about one a week. It's true. There are more "prophets" now than ever before, all of them claiming truth, claiming to speak for the people, most claiming to speak for God. The trouble is, most of them just seem to be speaking for themselves.

Given all these self-anointed prophets, it is obvious that the question must be raised as to real prophecy. Who are the true and who are the false prophets? "Will the prophets of God please stand up?" Some would insist, though, that we leave things pretty much like they are.

"Shouldn't we look for the good in everybody?"

"If someone says he or she is a prophet, well, okay."

"It would be rather illiberal of us to presume to judge among the prophets anyway."

And so the prophets continue to parade before us — Ayatollahs carrying assault rifles, revolutionaries wearing berets, evangelists waving Bibles — all claiming to speak the truth, to speak for the people, to speak for God.

Now the interesting thing is that Scripture is quite aware of this question of true and false prophets. Biblical faith is much more rigorous than we are.

The covenant people are called to discern not only among spirits, but among prophets. For if a prophet is truly from God, and speaks on God's behalf, then we are called to listen and respond. The prophetic word changes the world and creates a new world by its power. So, to discern among the prophets is really to raise the questions of covenant identity. Who are we? How shall we live?

Who *are* God's prophets? In our Old Testament lesson, these questions are addressed directly. Within Deuteronomy is a deep concern about who we are as God's people — and, therefore, who the true prophets are.

Who is a prophet? Our lesson instructs the covenant people how to discern among the prophets. A prophet, Deuteronomy proclaims, will (first of all) be like Moses.

> *"The Lord your God will raise up for you a prophet like me from among you."*

Moses, who spoke these words, was a leader of Israel and the prototype of the prophets. So if we are going to look in the right direction for a true prophet of the Lord, it is important to know how it was that Moses was the prophet *par excellence*.

What was it about Moses that made him a prophet? Well, for one thing, Moses stood as an intermediary between God and the people. When God appeared before Israel at the holy mountain, the presence of the Lord was unbearably overpowering.

> *"And you came near and stood at the foot of the mountain, while the mountain burned with fire to the heart of heaven, wrapped in darkness, cloud, and gloom. Then the Lord spoke to you out of the midst of the fire . . ."*

It was too awesome, too overwhelming, too much divine presence. So Moses becomes the prophet who stands between God and the people. But notice this! The prophet intercedes on behalf of the whole covenant, for all the people of God. Amos will call Israel to repentance. He will say to all the people, "Let justice roll down like waters, and righteousness like an everflowing stream." Hosea will speak of God's steadfast love for Israel. Even after they have turned away, God will still love them as a mother loves her children. Jesus will proclaim the Good News of God's reign to all of Israel and will seek out those who are lost. A prophet is concerned for God's people. A prophet *loves* God's people — even while speaking for the burning anger of God, a prophet calls the covenant people to be reconciled to their merciful God.

A prophet, like Moses, is also a law-giver. Deuteronomy portrays Moses as giving instruction to the people as to God's law. This prophet is teaching Israel how to live righteously before the Lord. There are to be three cities of sanctuary where one who has killed someone accidentally may find haven. Distinctions between foods which are clean and unclean are taught to the people. Above all, the Ten Commandments of the Lord God are proclaimed before the people by Moses, the prophet of the Lord. And a prophet like Moses will be raised up from among the people: another law-giver, who will teach God's people at the beginning of the new age. We will see him in the midst of the people, up on the mountain, saying,

> "Blessed are the poor in spirit
> for theirs is the Kingdom of heaven.
> Blessed are those who mourn,
> for they shall be comforted . . .
> Blessed are those who hunger and thirst for righteousness,
> for they shall be satisfied."

A prophet like Moses will bring the law of God to Israel. There will be a new Moses who will bring forth a new covenant.

A prophet like Moses will also lead the covenant people from bondage. The prophet whom God raises up will again act to save Israel. Just as Moses led the children of Israel through the Sea, so a new prophet will once again work to set the people free. There will be a new Passover which will set us free and establish us as God's own. This prophet like Moses will go on before us, from death to new life, from shame to glory. You know that Passover — that *new* Passover — with its crown of thorns and flogging, that walk to Calvary, the victim carrying his cross. Then, "they nailed him to the tree" and later on, "they laid him in the tomb." And for three days, only the sign of Jonah. But our new Moses went on before us. "And on the third day was raised from the dead." From death to life. By the power of God — that Exodus God — the cross stands empty and he is not in the tomb. "He is risen, and he is going on before you . . ." Yes, that's the One. The prophet of the Lord, a new Moses, God's only Son! Bringing with him a host of people, through the waters . . . from death to life, freed from bondage.

The prophet of the Lord will also show another clear sign of that calling. God's prophets will not serve other gods. They will not speak in the name of other gods, but only of the God of Israel. So we won't hear a prophet of the Lord speak as if God cares only for America. It wasn't a prophet of the Lord who delivered the invocation at the Orange Bowl half-time while a football field-size American flag was unfurled. There weren't many prophets of the Lord at those White House services blessing our policies in Vietnam. And you are not likely to see a prophet of God making more of "Independence Sunday" than Easter.

The prophets of the Lord serve no other gods, not those of this nation or any other. The new covenant in Jesus Christ is not a national covenant, not a racial covenant, not an ideological covenant. These gods have been cast down from their throne by the death and resurrection of Christ. And a faithful prophet will speak only in the name of this one true Lord.

There is one other test of a true prophet. Moses announces a quite obvious way to discern among the prophets. Has the word of the prophet come true? Has that word come to pass? It seems simple enough, but it's a test some people will avoid applying to their favorite "prophet" because they have become too secure within the would-be world. In James Michener's novel *Space,* an unscrupulous character, Dr. Strabismus, preys on people's anxieties by prophecying the arrival of visitors from outer space. Only his organization, Universal Space Associates, has been able to establish contact with the "little men" and therefore prevent a global disaster. Money pours in to Strabismus as he predicts and then postpones their arrival repeatedly. One of his most ardent supporters, ironically, is the wife of a U.S. senator who is a strong proponent of American space efforts. Along with many others, the senator's wife cannot bring herself to conclude about Strabismus what Moses cautioned concerning prophets: " . . . if the word does not come to pass . . . the prophet has spoken it presumptuously." Has the word come true? If not, it is not worthy, it is not the word of the Lord.

Now a word has been spoken to us. It is a prophetic word which claims to be "Good News," spoken by the new Moses to the new Israel.

*I am the good shepherd;
I know my own and my own know me, . . .
and I lay down my life for the sheep . . .
So there shall be one flock, one shepherd.*

His word is true. It can be trusted. It will never fail.

Epiphany 5
Job 7:1-7

"Job" Is Our Name Too

"Have you considered my servant Job?" God asked Satan in the heavenly court. This "blameless and upright man, who fears God and turns away from evil?" Well, Satan considered Job all right. But he only considered him a God-fearing man because he was being blessed. Remove all that blessing, Satan argued, and Job's piety will crumble and he will curse you. So the agreement is made between God and Satan; only Job's life must not be taken away. But everything else is of Job's is negotiable — family, servants, house, possessions. All of it. Job is then afflicted with sores covering his body, and he falls on the ground in lament.

"... the Lord gave and the Lord has taken away; blessed be the name of the Lord."

And the author of the Book of Job comments, "In all this Job did not sin..."

Whatever else this drama of Job is about, it is a tale of innocent suffering. Job is a righteous person, who fears God and who rejects evil. Yet within the scope of a couple dozen verses, we see Job transformed from the embodiment of Jewish blessing to the most tragic example of curse. Loss of family, wealth, and then even reputation come swiftly to Job. Yet he is innocent. God agrees, Satan agrees, and Job maintains his innocence throughout. The story is one of a good person suffering evil. And in this story Job represents all those who suffer as he does, innocent victims of evil. The innocent *do* suffer, and Job is not an exception: he is the symbol of all who suffer undeserved evil.

In one evening newscast you can sample the whole span of this innocent suffering. The lead story may be the Middle East again, with coverage of the casualties of the latest shelling. The religion is different, but we watch the same grief of families who have lost loved ones. It was just a matter of where the rockets fell. Even the wailing laments sound the same. It is the lament of Job. Later in the newscast, we look at an infant in need of a liver transplant. The jaundice is immediately apparent, confirming the life-or-death issue. Another innocent sufferer is joined in fellowship to brother Job. Finally, we see the coverage of an armed robbery. The brutal violence was "senseless," the reporter states, and three shoppers lie dead in a convenience store. Their loved ones join in the questions raised by Job: "Why has this happened? Why does God permit this evil to occur?" Every night it's like that. The innocent suffering. We read about it, we watch it live and in color, and it happens to us and our loved ones. The innocent joining with Job in a fellowship of suffering.

Almost as inevitable as the suffering of Job is what happens next. Job's friends come to him to interpret the meaning of his distress. "You have sinned," they announce, "and the sooner you repent, the sooner your fortunes will change." Job's friends are quite orthodox in their diagnosis of the suffering they see. All this "ill-fortune" is really curse, God's judgment for wrong-doing. Only some awful sin could result in such awful suffering. Therefore, Job is a sinner. His suffering gives him away. God is angry with him. The only other explanation would be that God is unjust, and that is unthinkable. "Does God pervert justice?" they ask. So they attack Job for his stiff-necked refusal to confess his guilt and admit his wrong. Their argument makes God into a cosmic computer, programmed to hand out retribution on a scale equal to the evil committed. Minor suffering equals minor guilt, and Job-level misfortune clearly points to God-only-knows what sort of sinfulness. But for Job's friends, the divine computer is also programmed for the elimination of such suffering. Admit your faults and there is a good chance things will take a quick turn for the better. And in response to Job's questioning as to why the universe works this way, his friendly advisers assure him that God's ways are beyond knowing. After spending days explaining to Job how the divine machine works and why he got caught in it, they piously report that God is a mystery. But for Job, this explanation is untrue. He has not sinned, and yet he suffers. He knows this, and we know it too.

Now what is odd here is that we hear the argument of Job's friends and we accept it. We don't particularly like the way their computer print-out reads, but we accept it as gospel truth anyway. So whenever suffering is encountered, it is a sure thing that God's wrath is being displayed right in front of us. But we're not so different than most everybody when it comes to this solidarity with Job's friends. It's rare when some *other* explanation of suffering is given! A mother looks down at her child lying sick in bed. The fever is high, cheeks are flushed . . . there is some sort of infection. And in the midst of the other feelings at that moment, the mother bumps into a guilt problem. "If only I had done this . . . or that . . . then my baby wouldn't be in this condition." The mother has accepted the thinking of Job's friends. The commuters on the train into the city glance out the window and look down at the ghetto passing by under the elevated. "Those idle people," some think, "if they weren't so lazy they would get themselves out of there." Job's friends ride the el every day, to work and back to the suburbs. Such misfortune as this poverty is admissible evidence that those people are guilty somehow.

We even apply the advice of Job's friends to ourselves. Some of us here have been through that eternity in the doctor's office, waiting for the tests to be done. We lie there on the hard examination bed and pass the time counting the number of holes in the ceiling tiles. Finally the doctor returns and we look up for some news. It's bad . . . and we're going to need to take time off from work, lose weight, give up smoking. Have you noticed, in yourself or a friend, how this kind of crisis can eat away at a person's self-esteem? It is as if we only have value when we are capable of working. And if that worth is threatened by sickness, then we're not sure who we are, or if we are worth anything. Job's friends have just gained another companion. We are continually tempted to apply this "wisdom" to our own sufferings and to the sufferings of those around us. Innocent suffering becomes a contradiction in terms.

It is precisely in such a situation that we see Job at his lowest. That contradiction sits there with him on the ash heap. It entangles him. On one hand, he asks for vindication; rather, *demands* it of God.

> *"Oh that I knew where I might find him,*
> *that I may come even to his seat! —*
> *... Would he contend with me in the greatness of his*
> *power?*
> *No he would give heed to me.*

If Job could only get the Lord God subpoenaed into court, there would be acquittal for Job. More than anything, he wants vindication from his God.

But at the same time, Job is torn by the anger he feels towards his accusers and their "wisdom." He calls them "worthless physicians" and then levels a further insult: "Your maxims are proverbs of ashes . . . " Job is in a fury because of the "prescriptions" of his friends. Yet at the same time he is counting on that wisdom to save him. Surely, if he can bring God to the tribunal, he can get the sentence dismissed and a "not guilty" ruling. Then he will be restored.

This self-contradiction that has caught Job is powerful and beguiling. We come across the pitfall again and again. It is one of the central struggles of human life. A poor family does not buy the maxim that their poverty is their fault, and so they work twice, three times, as hard as other people in order to disprove it. But no matter how hard they work, they drag the "wisdom" along with them.

Have you ever met someone who is blessed with a good measure of success in this life, but who seems driven to keep succeeding? It just may be that the person has been struggling for years to overcome some childhood events that still define who he or she is, afraid that if the world knew of the poverty or abuse of that child, that world would declare the adult "not worthy." Do you know someone caught in that trap? The "no-matter-how-hard-I-work-and-succeed,-it's-still-not-enough" trap. Are you, perhaps, caught in it yourself? Are we in that pitfall with brother Job . . . ? And if we are, how in the world do we get out?

For Job, getting out of that trapnet involved an epiphany . . . the appearance of the Almighty God. God comes before Job . . . and the presence of the Lord and the word of the Lord are overpowering to this suffering soul. Out of the whirlwind, God responds to Job:

> "*Where were you when I laid the foundation of the earth?*
> *Tell me, if you have understanding.*"

Question after question challenges any claim Job might have to meet God as an equal —

> "*Have you entered into the springs of the sea,*
> *or walked in the recesses of the deep?*
> *Have the gates of death been revealed to you,*
> *or have you seen the gates of deep darkness?*
> *Can you bind the chains of the Pleiades,*
> *or loose the chains of Orion?*"

And, of course, Job must answer, "No." Only God is holy and has created all things. So Job confesses to God that he repents in dust and ashes. He repents, not of his claim to innocence, but of his presumptuousness. For he had sought to make God deal with him on the basis of some very human "wisdom." But note this! God now, at the end, still declares Job innocent. God has not asked Job to reject what he has known about himself. But as for Job's friends, they are declared guilty by God.

> *You have not spoken of me what is right,*
> *as my servant Job has.*

It is Job's friends who now must repent, for they were wrong. Their "wisdom" was foolishness.

So, Job is restored to health and prosperity. He is given twice as much as he had before. "And the Lord blessed the latter days of Job more than his beginning." Job heads off to a restoration meal with "all who had known him before." And his friends also head off, in a different direction, to offer sacrifice for their falsehoods about God. So, here on this old ash heap, it looks like only we are left.

Except, we don't have to stay here either. You see, what Job did not know was that God planned to appear in another way to the rest of us. There would be a different kind of epiphany. The holiness would be present, but many would miss it. In the fullness of time, God would appear, in our Job-like flesh, as a Servant. And the Servant would suffer and disclose the very pain of God: the

Redeemer Job prayed for would come, and suffer, and die. And what Job didn't know, over there feasting with all his acquaintances, and what we *do* know, is that God has accepted that suffering on the Cross. It was for us. All our sufferings are couched within the suffering of the Lord. And we know that our Redeemer lives.

Transfiguration
2 Kings 2:1-12a

Behold! Chariots of Fire!

Elisha had been with Elijah for what seemed like a long time. It began in the most dramatic way: Elijah lamenting that the people of Israel had all forsaken the covenant, everyone in Israel bowing the knee to false gods; Elijah complaining, "And I, even I only, am left." But the Lord God refused to let the prophet just hide out there in the wilderness. So Elijah was sent back to do battle against the idolatry of Israel and to anoint a new king. And Elijah was also given a successor who would be anointed to continue God's struggle with a rebellious people. So Elijah found Elisha plowing in his father's field and threw his mantle on the young man. And Elisha followed Elijah and ministered to him. Like a son and his father were these two prophets of the Lord.

But it was now coming to the time when the Lord was to take Elijah away. Soon Elisha would be left behind to carry on the mission entrusted to the two of them. As they walked together on this last journey, they passed by three of the holiest shrines of Israel. And at each place, Elijah said to Elisha, "Tarry here, I pray you . . ." — at Gilgal, and Bethel, and at Jericho. Perhaps the request was to make the parting easier on Elisha. "Stay here in the company of the prophets at this shrine." That way the parting might be less painful. But each time Elijah made his request, Elisha said, "As the Lord lives, and as you yourself live, I will not leave you." And so at each holy place this little drama took place, once, twice, three times:

"Tarry here."

"I will not leave you."

So together still, they head for the Jordan and the wilderness on the other side.
There is something commendable about the young man's devotion. He knows that a final parting will come soon. But he stubbornly follows the great prophet, not knowing where he would be led or what would happen.
The call to ministry is always like that. The mantle is placed on a person and a disciple is made. Being a disciple seems to create more questions than answers. And there are repeated occasions when a way out of that call is offered. It is something like the "call" you experience when you fall in love, and the relationship deepens with all the time spent together . . . and apart. The "call" soon becomes, "Will you marry me?" And the answers have a way of evolving, from, "Oh, be serious!" to "Yes! I will!" There are times when a way out seems quite attractive, and some take it. As a matter of fact, it *does* take a kind of disciple-like stubbornness for covenant love to grow into a faithful marriage. There is a call in that journey, like the call to ministry; like Elisha's call to follow Elijah and to follow the Lord God. So they leave the shrines behind and set out toward the Jordan and the wilderness.
At the Jordan, Elijah stands there with Elisha. It is time to cross. Elijah takes his mantle and strikes the water, and it is parted "till the two of them could go over on dry ground." And they cross the River Jordan. It seems as though Israel's whole life with the God of the covenant can be summed up by these "crossings" of the waters. Just think about it! The Lord God acts to free a little band of slaves in Egypt and leads them to freedom across the sea. After the forty years of wandering in the wilderness, the tribes of Israel come to the Jordan and the Ark is carried out to the middle of the Jordan, stopped, and turned back, and the people cross on dry ground. Much, much later, John the Baptizer appears, at this Jordan, inviting Israel to be baptized for repentance. And Jesus comes before John, is baptized in the Jordan, and there is a voice from heaven: "This is my beloved Son." Israel seems always led to a water crossing, from bondage to freedom, from wilderness to Promised Land, from sin to repentance. And finally, in Jesus Christ, a crossing from death to new life.
So the Jordan is for God's people a boundary, a boundary and

a place of passing. Joshua and the people, Elijah and Elisha, John and Jesus . . . all making a passage, led by God. Those sorts of "crossings" happen to us sometimes. There is a glimpse of what that sort of passage is like. A young couple leaves the little church college out in the sticks and heads off for their first jobs in the city. There is a scary feeling to the move, and they know they can't go back. So there they go, onto the interstate, pulling the U-Haul trailer behind the old Plymouth. It's Jordan-crossing time. Or think what happened over and over again in Vietnam. Two soldiers, with totally different backgrounds, different races maybe, come through a hellish battle together. Both of them pressing into the earth as the shells come in, find themselves bonded, one to the other. It is almost a blood bond; they have become like brothers. A passage has occurred, a kind of water crossing, like the Jordan. And they can never go back.

This kind of passage always involved that "you-can't-go-back" awareness. A young man is having kidney failure. Every week he gets hooked up to that machine, but it just gets worse. Then we hear about the operation. His sister has donated one of her own kidneys for her kid brother. Both of them will live, but a Jordan has been crossed and they will never be the same. There is a new, deeper bond between them that will endure, for they have made the passage together. It is like that to cross the Jordan. For Israel, and (in our baptisms) for us. A passage, together, knowing that you cannot go back. New life lies ahead. And the Lord Jesus calling us to come and follow him.

So they cross the Jordan, Elijah and Elisha. They walk across the damp river rocks and come to the wilderness. And after they have passed over, Elisha makes a last request of Elijah:

"I pray you, let me inherit a double share of your spirit."

He is asking for the share of inheritance due the first born. This is not an expression of greed; it is a plea that he become Elijah's successor. Elisha is asking that the spirit which was given to Elijah be his now, transferred from the prophet to the disciple. He is requesting the rights of the first born.

At this point, we are on more familiar ground. Most of us here have been a party to these kinds of rituals of conferral. We stand in the driveway and watch as a son or daughter motors away for the first time alone. The keys are no longer in our possession. They have been given away, and with them has been given a double share of our spirit. There is a very special kind of conferral when a business becomes a family business. The signs all used to read "... and Son." But now we're seeing "... *and Daughter,*" too! And at some point in the life of this family business, the responsibility passes over to the younger generation. At some time or another, the daughter or son is given a double share of the spirit. Or consider what happens in a close family when the daughter first has a baby. From the moment of the delivery, even while the new grandparents are peering proudly through the glass wall of the nursery, there is a conferral going on. "Mother" is becoming "grandmother," and a new mother is assuming that central role. The change affects everyone, and identities permanently shift. And when the ritual happens with love and sensitivity, there is the gift of a double share of the spirit. We know of these things. They are times of grace, for us as well as for Elijah and that disciple of his, Elisha.

But for those of us who have been baptized, the grace of this conferral has already come. When we went through the waters of our Jordan, we came up as "first born," sons and daughters of God. Now we have been born anew, made a part of the family of Christ, "given the keys," with a new authority, and a new identity. It is good to return thanks to our God, for we have been given a double share of the Spirit of Christ. And whatever else this festival of the Transfiguration means, it points to that conferral of Sonship given at our Lord's baptism. Up there, on "a very high mountain," with Moses and Elijah, the heavenly voice repeats the words of the Jordan: "This is my beloved Son." This first born of the new humanity, shining with the radiance of God's presence ... this Savior turns to us and invites us to share in his life and his service. And we are offered a double share of his Spirit. We, too, have become "first born."

The request is made by Elisha. And Elijah answers, "If you see me ... it shall be so."

And as they still went on and talked, behold, a chariot of fire and horses of fire separated the two of them. And Elijah went up by a whirlwind into heaven.

There was a point beyond which Elisha could not go. The boundary this time could not be crossed. A presence of the glory of God stopped the disciple from following Elijah. Just as on the high mountain, when our Lord was transfigured before Peter and James and John, "and his garments became glistening, intensely white." There is a separation that such glory brings. We cannot cross over. But we stand in awe and wonder at what has happened.

In the very human events of our lives, we come upon times something like this, when there is great glory and we must remain behind. A father and mother proudly proceed down the aisle to the glorious organ music. Behind them come the bride and groom. And after loving words of support and blessing, the parents sit down and watch the transformation happening before their eyes. A boundary has been established in the midst of the praise and rejoicing. There is a necessary separation. But we watch in awe and wonder at what has happened.

It happens, too, at a service of ordination — this separation. The young priest or minister was only our cousin or nephew before. But now, in the laying on of hands and in prayer, there is a transformation. A glorious time of rejoicing. But there is also a new separation, a boundary established and a kind of sadness. And we ponder with awe and wonder at what has happened. And it happens when one of the saints dies and we gather to honor the beloved sister or brother and to witness to the resurrection of Jesus Christ. We join in the singing of "For All the Saints" and hear the Good News proclaimed of the One who has gone to prepare a place for us. We pray the Shepherd Psalm and break the bread of life. And then we hear the words of committal and stand in awe and wonder at what has happened: this separation, this transformation, grief, and a vision of glory. There are boundary times in our life together when a chariot of fire separates us and prevents us from going on.

And so, Elisha is standing, trance-like, staring up into the heavens. "And he saw him no more," the story says. Moses and Elijah depart and the three disciples follow Jesus down toward Jerusalem. And at the ascension of the Lord, when he entered into glory, the disciples, like Elisha of old, were standing there, trance-like, staring up into the heavens. And on this day with its own chariots of fire, there is the question that always shatters these visions: "Why do you stand here looking into heaven?" Back from the wilderness with Elisha we come, wearing the Lord's mantle. First-born, now we are down from the mountain. We have seen the glory of the Lord, but now there are disciples to be made and baptized. There are prophetic words to be spoken and much service to be given before we too come into the presence of Christ's glory in that chariot of fire.